TYPE 2 DIABETES

COOKBOOK

365 Days of Balanced Diabetic Diet Recipes
For Newly Diagnosed Warriors! Love what you Eat!

28-DAY MEAL PLAN FOR BEGINNERS

By
JULIA MARTIN

ET CAT
PUBLISHING

YOUR VOICE MATTERS!

Book Editing, Design, and front Cover Design by ET Cat Publishing

Email: *et.publishing.us@gmail.com*

Table of Contents

INTRODUCTION TO TYPE-2 DIABETES   5

TYPE-2 DIABETES: CAUSES AND MEANING   5

DIFFERENCES BETWEEN TYPE 1 AND TYPE-2 DIABETES:

MANAGEMENT & TREATMENT   6

DIABETES-RELATED HEALTH PROBLEMS - ESPECIALLY AFTER 40-

50 YEARS OLD   7

NUTRIENTS AND DIABETES: 8

THE RELATIONSHIP   8

THE KEY TO SUCCESS FOR YOUR   8

DIABETIC DIET: NUTRITION BALANCE   8

FOOD TO LIMIT   8

YOUR MEAL PLAN TO TAKE CONTROL OF YOUR DIABETES   9

I HAVE DIABETES: WHAT CAN I EAT?   10

HOW TO FACE UP TO DIABETES: USEFUL TIPS   **10**

THE IMPORTANCE OF MINDFUL EATING   10

STRESS IS YOUR ENEMY!   10

STICK TO THE DIET PLAN   11

KEEP TRACK OF MEALS BY USING A FOOD DIARY   11

MOVE AND WALK AFTER EVERY MEAL   11

AVOID BINGES   11

DON'T DEPRIVE YOURSELF TOO MUCH   11

MEAL PLANNING HELPS   11

HEALTHY EATING   12

TIPS AND FAQ BEFORE YOU START   **12**

28-DAY MEAL PLAN   **15**

BREAKFAST   **17**

APPLE CINNAMON CAKE   18

(GRAIN-FREE)   18

SWEET ONION AND HAM OMELET   19

GRILLED CHEESE AND RYE TO START WITH ENERGY   19

AVOCADO TOAST BREAKFAST   20

KALE CHIPS   20

BLUEBERRY, CITRUS AND POPPY MUFFINS   21

ZUCCHINI AND YELLOW PEPPER SPECIAL SCRAMBLE   22

EGGS AND MIXED VEGETABLE   22

BERRIES & GREEK YOGURT SUNDAE   23

GNAMMY APPLE CHEDDAR MUFFINS   23

ORANGE-HONEY YOGURT   24

BROCCOLI PURÉE AND POTATO HASH BROWNS   24

CHOCO CHIP, BANANA AND PEANUT BUTTER CUP   25

ENGLISH MUFFIN MELTS   26

APPLE CINNAMON MUFFINS   26

SIDES & SALADS   **27**

ASPARAGUS AND BACON SALAD   28

MIXED GREENS AND PUMPKIN SEED SALAD   28

CHEESY CAULI BAKE   29

PAN-ROASTED BROCCOLI   29

SAUCY EGGPLANT AND CAPERS   30

SPICY GRAPEFRUIT AND AVOCADO SALAD   30

BRAISED FENNEL WITH WHITE WINE AND PARMESAN   31

CAPRESE SALAD   31

PARMESAN AND ZUCCHINI FRITTERS   32

SKILLET-ROASTED VEGGIES   32

TUNA, GREEN BEAN AND EGG SALAD   33

AUTUMN SLAW   33

ROASTED BEANS AND GREEN ONIONS   34

ENDIVE AND SWEET POTATO BAKE   34

POULTRY   **35**

CHICKEN ARROZ   36

CHICKEN BREAST IN RED WINE SAUCE   37

BALSAMIC CHICKEN AND VEGETABLE SKILLET   38

CITRUSY VEG CHICKEN ROAST   39

DIJON'D CHICKEN WITH ROSEMARY   40

CHICKEN CORDON BLEU   41

HAM AND CHEESE STUFFED CHICKEN BREASTS   42

CASHEW CHICKEN   43

HERBED CHICKEN AND SWEET POTATO BAKE   44

CHICKEN TUSCANY   45

RICOTTA AND TURKEY BELL PEPPERS   46

CRISPY ITALIAN CHICKEN WITH ZUCCHINI   47

HERB CRUSTED TURKEY BREASTS AND VEGGIES   48

SEAFOOD   **49**

PAN-SEARED SESAME-CRUSTED TUNA STEAKS   50

OVEN-ROASTED SALMON   51

BLACKENED SHRIMP   52

CRAB CAKES   53

BAKED SALMON WITH GARLIC PARMESAN TOPPING   54

CRUNCHY LEMON SHRIMP   55

USA SUSHI TUNA   56

LIME AND SEA BASS   57

SALMON WITH LEMON-THYME SLICES   58

SHRIMP AND HALIBUT SAUTÉ   59

PISTACHIOS AND HERB HALIBUT   60

FISHERMAN'S PIE   61

ROASTED COD AND FRENCH STEW   62

SHRIMP IN COCONUT CURRY   63

BEEF, PORK AND LAMB   **64**

PORK CHOPS POMODORO   65

PAN-SEARED SIRLOIN STEAK   66

BBQ PORK TACOS   67

BASIL MEATBALL BAKE   68

SLOW-COOKED ORANGE AND PORK SLAW   69

SWEET SHERRY'D PORK TENDERLOIN   70

BEER BRAISED BRISKET   71

QUICK & EASY STEAK TACOS   72

QUICK & EASY BEEF   73

HERB CRUSTED BAKED HAM   74

PARMESAN-CRUSTED PORK CHOPS   75

SWEET JERK PORK   76

SHERRY ROASTED BEEF AND PEPPER SAUCE   77

Julia Martin

LIME LAMB CHOPS	78
SOUPS, STEWS & CHILES	79
TILAPIA STEW WITH GREEN PEPPERS	80
KALE AND CAULIFLOWER SOUP	81
SALMON DILL SOUP	82
BEEF AND LENTIL SOUP	83
CHUNKY CHICKEN NOODLE SOUP	84
GREEN PEPPER SKILLET CHILI	84
ZUCCHINI AND TOMATO STEW	85
SOUTHWEST CHICKEN SOUP	85
SAUSAGE AND PEPPER SOUP	86
ITALIAN FISH STEW	87
DIJON'D CHICKEN WITH ROSEMARY	88
CREAM OF CHICKEN AND MUSHROOM SOUP	88
ITALIAN SAUSAGE SOUP	89
MEXICAN CHICKEN AND RICE	89
ONLY	90
VEGETARIAN MEALS	90
BALSAMIC BEAN SALSA SALAD	91
MUSHROOM CUTLETS WITH CREAMY SAUCE	91
SHERRY TOFU AND SPINACH STIR-FRY	92
CAULIFLOWER MUSHROOM RISOTTO	93
BRUSSELS SPROUT, AVOCADO, AND WILD RICE BOWL	94
FIRENZE PIZZA	95
BROCCOLI QUICHE (NO-CRUST)	96
VEGAN THAI RED CURRY	97
MOZZARELLA AND ARTICHOKE STUFFED SPAGHETTI SQUASH	98
BEET, GOAT CHEESE, AND WALNUT PESTO WITH ZUCCHINI	
NOODLES	99
SPINACH CASSEROLE	100
PIZZA STUFFED WITH MUSHROOMS	100
DESSERTS	**101**
LOW-CARBS ALMOND CAKE	102
VEGAN CHEESECAKE BITES (NO-BAKED)	103
OATMEAL COOKIES	104
CARAMEL PECAN PIE	105
CARROT CUPCAKES	106
POMEGRANATE AND NUT CHOCOLATE CLUSTERS	107
COFFEE BAKE	108
PEANUT BUTTER FUDGE BROWNIES	109
FROZEN CHOCOLATE MONKEY TREATS	110
PISTACHIO AND RICOTTA CHEESECAKE	110
DARK CHOCOLATE ALMOND BUTTER CUPS	111
SWIRLED CREAM CHEESE BROWNIES	111
DOUBLE-GINGER COOKIES	112
PEAR AND CINNAMON BAKE	112
CONCLUSIONS	**113**

Diabetes is one of the leading causes of premature death in the United States. According to records, approximately 1.4 million new cases of diabetes are diagnosed each year, and an estimated 8 million people are undiagnosed or uninformed about their condition. The estimated number of people over 18 with diagnosed and undiagnosed diabetes is more than 30.2 million. Diabetes is a disorder in which the body does not use the sugars in food in the typical way. Symptoms of diabetes in people vary, depending on the degree and complexity of the complication. When the body can't get sugar at the required place and time, this causes high blood sugar levels in the circulatory system, leading to complications such as nerve, kidney, eye, and cardiovascular disease. Sugar (glucose) is the preferred fuel for brain cells and muscles. However, it requires insulin to transport glucose into cells for use. But when insulin levels are low, there is not enough insulin to transport the sugar into the cells. This process causes high blood sugar levels. In the long run, the cells develop insulin resistance, and the focus now shifts to the pancreas, which is required to make more insulin to move sugar into the cells; despite this, more sugar remains in the blood. Because of the pressure on the pancreas, it will eventually "wear out," which means it will no longer secrete enough insulin to move sugar into the cells for energy.

Without ongoing, careful management, diabetes can lead to life-threatening complications, including blindness, foot amputations, and heart or kidney disease. It can lead to high blood sugar, increasing the risk of life-threatening complications, including strokes and heart disease.

Type 2 diabetes mellitus (T2DM) is one of the most common metabolic disorders worldwide. Its development is primarily caused by two main factors: defective insulin secretion by pancreatic cells and the inability of insulin-sensitive tissues to respond to insulin. Insulin release and action of insulin must precisely meet metabolic demand; therefore, the molecular mechanisms involved in insulin synthesis and release and the insulin response in tissues must be tightly regulated. Thus, defects in any of the mechanisms involved can lead to a metabolic imbalance, that leads to the pathogenesis of T2DM.

TYPE-2 DIABETES: CAUSES AND MEANING

According to the World Health Organization (WHO), diabetes mellitus is a chronic metabolic disease characterized by elevated blood glucose levels, leading to damage to the heart, vasculature, eyes, kidneys, and nerves, over time. More than 90% of diabetes mellitus are T2DM, a condition characterized by deficient insulin secretion by pancreatic islets, tissue insulin resistance (IR), and an inadequate compensatory secretory insulin response. Disease progression renders insulin secretion unable to maintain glucose homeostasis, producing hyperglycemia. Patients with T2DM are mostly characterized by being obese or having a higher percentage of body fat, distributed mainly in the abdominal region. In this condition, fatty tissue promotes IR through various inflammatory mechanisms, including increased free fatty acid (FFA) release and deregulation of adipokines. The primary causes of T2DM are the increase in obesity worldwide, sedentary lifestyles, high-calorie diets, and an aging population, which have quadrupled the incidence and prevalence of T2DM (Galicia-Garcia et al. 2020).

Receiving a diagnosis of type 2 diabetes doesn't mean you were "bad." It doesn't mean you brought it on yourself. And it doesn't mean you should be punished or judged.

Other people eat, drink, and watch TV like you and don't have diabetes. It means they have a different genetic makeup than you do. You may have inherited the genes linked to your risk of developing diabetes from your mother and father or your grandparents.

While there is a strong genetic link to type 2 diabetes, having a family history does not automatically mean you will develop it. Lifestyle factors such as diet and exercise are even more important than your DNA. The genetic mutations that cause type 2 diabetes can be controlled by what you eat and how much exercise you get. Those with the genetic makeup that is more resistant to diabetes should also be careful about eating poorly and spending most of their time on the couch. They too, may develop diabetes.

When your doctor says, "You have type 2 diabetes," it's usually after blood tests. Diabetes is characterized by blood sugar levels that are higher than normal. This means that your fasting blood sugar level (when you wake up in the morning) and your postprandial blood sugar level (2 hours after eating) is high.

DIFFERENCES BETWEEN TYPE 1 AND TYPE-2 DIABETES: MANAGEMENT & TREATMENT

Most people know that there are two types of diabetes, but not everybody understands the difference between them. The main difference between the three types of diabetes is that type 1 diabetes, also known as insulin-dependent diabetes, is an autoimmune disorder that often begins in childhood. It's a condition in which the immune system attacks and destroys insulin-producing cells of the pancreas, or the pancreas cells don't work effectively, leading to reduced insulin production. Without insulin, glucose from Carbohydrate foods cannot enter the cells. This causes glucose to build up in the bloodstream, leaving your body's cells and tissues starved for energy.

Type 2, also known as adult-onset diabetes, is the most common form of diabetes. Type 2 diabetes is largely diet-related and can be caused by several factors. One factor that can cause this type of diabetes is when the pancreas makes less insulin. The second possible cause could be that the body becomes resistant to insulin. This means that the pancreas makes insulin, but it does not use it efficiently. In type 1 and type 2 diabetes, blood sugar levels may be too high because the body does not produce or use insulin properly. Diabetes can be managed, and diabetic patients can still live relatively "normal" lives.

Gestational diabetes is an elevated glucose level during pregnancy. This usually resolves once the baby is born and your blood sugar returns to normal. But you have a greater chance of developing type 2 diabetes later in life. During pregnancy, uncontrolled blood sugar levels usually result in larger, heavier babies who have a higher risk of being obese and becoming diabetic when they get older.

Because type 1 diabetes is generic, blood tests are necessary for diagnosis. However, blood tests that determine the likelihood of type 1 may only be recommended by doctors when a patient begins to show symptoms. An A1C screening tests blood sugar levels between two and three months and is typically used to diagnose type 1 and type 2 diabetes.

There are three main types of diabetes. Although all three involve high blood sugar levels, the underlying causes are different. All three are diagnosed using the same blood tests:

- Fasting blood sugar: A blood test determines your blood sugar level when you wake up before eating or drinking anything. It is considered high if the blood sugar reading is above 5.6 mmol per liter.

- HbA1c: A blood test that determines your average blood sugar level over the past three months. A reading above 6.5% means you have diabetes.

- Glucose tolerance test: This test takes place over three hours. Your fasting blood glucose level will be tested, and then you will be given a glucose solution to drink. Your blood sugar levels will be tested every 30-60 minutes to see how efficiently your body removes sugar from your blood. If your blood sugar is above 7.8 mmol per liter 2 hours after drinking the solution, you most likely have diabetes.

Unlike type 1 diabetes, which is generic, there are many ways to prevent type 2 diabetes. Ways to prevent type 2 diabetes include:
- A healthy diet
- Quitting smoking
- Increasing fiber intake

- Exercise and weight management
- Maintaining an average blood pressure
- Keeping alcohol consumption low
Diabetes treatment
Type 1 diabetes has no cure; however, it can be managed by injecting insulin into the fatty tissue under the skin. Managing type 1 diabetes is maintaining healthy blood glucose levels before and after meals. The patient must understand the blood glucose requirement and maintain it at all times to enjoy good health and prevent or delay complications of diabetes.
The different means of injecting insulin include:
- High-pressure air-jet injector
- Syringe
- Insulin pump
Other measures needed to treat type 1 and type 2 diabetes include:
- Careful meal planning
- Healthy eating
- Healthy weight management
- Frequent blood sugar testing
- Regular exercise
- Medication.
- Glucagon for emergency management of hypoglycemia

DIABETES-RELATED HEALTH PROBLEMS - ESPECIALLY AFTER 40-50 YEARS OLD

About one in four individuals over 60 years of age have diabetes. You're more likely to suffer from its harsh effects if you develop this condition.
Some health problems can be made worse by aging and a poor lifestyle. While you can't turn back the clock, you can take steps to lessen the chance of future difficulties or at least delay them. Talk to your doctor to assure you that your diabetes is under control. Stick to your treatment plan, take your medication, watch your food, and be more active.
All of these actions will go a long way toward helping you live a healthier and longer life. Here's a closer look at the health
impacts of diabetes and aging.

EYE PROBLEMS
Some eye problems can be caused by aging and diabetes. Cataracts, glaucoma, and retinopathy are among them. Each of these conditions can cause severe vision problems and possibly blindness. Visit your eye doctor at least once a year for a dilated eye test. This test allows you to see the inside of your eye more clearly. Don't wait until your next appointment if you detect any changes in your eyes or vision.

GUM DISEASE
If you don't take care of your teeth, and as you age, gum disease is more likely to develop, which can cause an infection in your gums and other tissues nearby. Gum disease is more likely to occur if you have diabetes. It reduces your ability to fight infections, including oral infections. Untreated gum disease can lead to tooth loss. Fortunately, there are many things you can do to avoid these problems. Brush your teeth twice a day. Floss at least once a day. Also, use an antibacterial mouthwash daily. Maintaining a healthy sugar level and going to your dentist every six months will help you avoid dental problems. Call the dentist right away if you see any signs of illness, such as red, swollen, or bleeding gums.

FLU AND PNEUMONIA
If you have diabetes and get sick with the ordinary flu, you're more likely to have significant complications, especially if you are over 65 and have diabetes. Because diabetes and aging decrease your immune system, you'll be less equipped to fight off infections. Pneumonia, sinus infections, bronchitis, and ear infections are all possible complications of the flu.
Complications can lead to hospitalization and even death, in the most severe cases. The flu can aggravate diabetes by raising blood sugar levels. It can also affect your appetite, and if you don't eat enough, your blood sugar levels will drop.

DEMENTIA AND ALZHEIMER'S

Both mental disorders are linked to aging Both mental disorders are linked to aging and diabetes. High blood sugar levels can damage various organs, including the brain. Alzheimer's disease can affect memory, the ability to learn, reasoning ability, judgment, and the ability to perform daily chores over time. Doctors are still learning a lot about the connection, but the best approach to lowering your risk, is to keep your diabetes under control.

NUTRIENTS AND DIABETES: THE RELATIONSHIP

People who have diabetes have excess blood sugar. Therefore, managing diabetes means managing your blood sugar level by eating foods which are rich in particular nutrients or injecting insulin. The nutrients in what you eat are linked to your overall well-being. The right nutrient choices will help you control your blood sugar levels. Eating foods rich in the proper nutrients is one of the main things you can do to help control diabetes. There is no specific "diabetes diet" for diabetes, but a dietitian can work with you to design an eating plan to guide you on what types of food to eat and what snacks to have with meals. A nutritious diet consists of:
- 20% of calories from Protein
- 40%-60% from Carbohydrates
- 30% or fewer calories from Fat

Your diet should also be low in salt, cholesterol, and added sugars.

Contrary to popular belief, eating a little sugar does not cause problems for most people who have diabetes. However, it is important to control the amount of sugar you consume and make sure it is part of a balanced diet.

In general, each meal should have the following nutrients:
- 2-5 choices (or up to 60 grams) of Carbohydrates
- A choice of Protein
- A certain amount of Fat

THE KEY TO SUCCESS FOR YOUR DIABETIC DIET: NUTRITION BALANCE

A healthy diet for diabetes is the same as the recommended healthy diet for the general population. We often deviate from the official dietary guidelines by enjoying too many fatty and sugary foods. Living with type 2 diabetes means adhering to these recommendations more strictly.

It may seem like you need to make some pretty significant changes to your shopping list and eating habits, but there's a good chance you'll find it easier than you think. It all starts with a balanced plate.

The goal is to fill half of your plate with vegetables. Try to eat primarily non-starchy vegetables, such as spinach, kale, green beans, and carrots. You don't have to avoid vegetables that contain a few extra Carbs, but limit the amount of butternut squash, and corn you eat.

Once you've served your veggies, add a Protein food such as meat, fish, chicken, or legumes to fill just a quarter of your plate. Your body's Protein requirements are surprisingly small. The ideal portion is about the size of the palm of your hand.

Finally, add Carbohydrates to your plate. They should take up the remaining quarter. Aim for whole grain foods and unprocessed Carbohydrates such as brown rice, barley, and sweet potatoes.

Fats are also essential and are most likely used in the cooking process. Fats like olive oil add flavor and nutrition to your meals. Your food doesn't have to be fat-free, but you don't want to overdo it.

FOOD TO LIMIT

Let's get the bad news out of the way first. You should avoid these foods altogether or limit them when you need to control your blood sugar levels. These are foods that everyone should limit, not just people with diabetes. They are foods that cause a spike in blood sugar levels, increase inflammation in general, and impact the amount of fat in the blood.

Refined sugar is a definite NO. Try to wean yourself off sugar in your tea and coffee. This is much easier than just stopping. It allows your taste buds to adjust slowly. Before you know it, you won't be enjoying tea or coffee with sugar in it.

Also, keep an eye out for sugary foods and snacks like chocolates, sweets, cold drinks, baked foods, and desserts. Your body does not need to do much work to extract the sugar from these foods, so it is released very quickly into the bloodstream. This causes a quick, high spike in blood sugar levels.

Remember that all Carbohydrates are digested in their simplest form - glucose. This doesn't mean you should avoid all starchy foods. But you should be wary of refined ones. The more processing your food has undergone, the less your body has to do to extract energy from it and the higher your blood sugar spike will be. Avoid all foods made with white flour, such as white bread, pizza, and cookies.

Foods that contain a lot of saturated fat are also problematic. They may not cause a spike in blood glucose levels, but they have been implicated in the development of type 2 diabetes. They also cause inflammation in the body and increase levels of bad cholesterol. Meat fat, chicken skin, full cream dairy products, cheese, and coconut oil are delicious but must be limited.

YOUR MEAL PLAN TO TAKE CONTROL OF YOUR DIABETES

Combine your balanced plate with the recommended foods, and start a healthy diet for your whole family.

Try to eat breakfast, lunch, and dinner every day. Your meal pattern should align with your medication. The goal of the medication is to reduce blood sugar levels. If you take it and don't eat well, you may find yourself experiencing low blood sugar.

When you eat regular meals that contain foods from all food groups, it becomes easier to control your blood sugar levels. Meals like this provide your body with enough energy to get you through the day, enough Protein to build and repair body tissues, and enough micronutrients to keep you healthy.

Because your blood sugar levels change according to what you eat, your diet is the key to managing diabetes. A healthy diet can also help you lose weight. A lower body weight improves your body's sensitivity to insulin, enhancing how you metabolize sugar.

In some cases, a healthy diet and regular exercise can help reduce the amount of medication you need to control your blood sugar levels. But always talk to your doctor before changing your medication.

A newly diagnosed type 2 diabetes condition can be overwhelming. It can feel like you are drowning in conflicting information. Everyone seems to have an opinion. Take your health into your own hands and formulate a plan that works for you. Use the advice from your doctor and dietitian, then sit down and figure out how you will move forward with your condition.

The successful management of your type 2 diabetes depends on your commitment—plan to succeed in taking control of your blood glucose levels. Once you have a plan, it is easier to see your way. The sugary, fatty foods that may have held your attention before become less appealing when your body receives all of the energy and nutrition.

Use the comprehensive 28-day meal plan we have compiled to get you started. We have created 100+ delicious and healthy recipes that you and your family will love, to go with the program. You and your family's health can improve with just a little bit of planning and effort in the kitchen.

I HAVE DIABETES: WHAT CAN I EAT?

Food Group	Recommended Foods
Vegetable	Cauliflower, cucumber, baby marrow, green beans, mushrooms, tomatoes, gem squash, carrots, cabbage, broccoli, celery, sweet peppers, lettuce, onions, garlic, spinach,
Fat	Canola oil, olive oil, macadamia nut oil, nuts, avocado pears, seeds, nut butters, low-fat margarine Limit: butter, cream, mayonnaise, salad dressing
Protein	Lean beef, skinless chicken, pork without the fat, soya, legumes, fish, eggs Limit: cheese, lamb/mutton
Milk	Fat-free milk, low-fat milk, evaporated milk, soya milk, low-fat plain yoghurt, low-fat buttermilk, fat-free plain yoghurt
Fruit	Apples, strawberries, peaches, nectarines, oranges, pears, mandarins, grapefruit, lemons, blueberries, cherries
Carbohydrate	Seeded bread, whole wheat bread, rye bread, sourdough bread, dried beans such as butter beans, whole wheat crackers, chickpeas, lentils, barley, quinoa, bulgur wheat, brown rice, sweet potatoes, whole pasta made from durum wheat or semolina, wheat pasta, low-fat low-sugar muesli, rolled oats, fiber-rich breakfast cereals

HOW TO FACE UP TO DIABETES: USEFUL TIPS

Managing diabetes seems easier in theory than in practice Following an effective dietary regimen to control blood glucose levels will not work unless certain essential habits are developed. Most patients get off to a good start in their diabetes management. However, they gradually lose the motivation and consistency to follow the new lifestyle and diet in order to achieve better health. As a result, they cause irreparable damage to their health. So, it is essential to practise the following habits and stick to them to be successful with diabetes:

THE IMPORTANCE OF MINDFUL EATING

Mindful Eating for Pre-diabetes and Diabetes is a realistic mind-body approach that focuses on awareness of your beliefs, habits, thoughts, feelings, and bodily sensations rather than rigid nutritional guidelines and strict exercise regimens. Take control of your eating and health habits as you learn to listen to and understand your inner expert.

Even if you have pre-diabetes or diabetes, enjoy every meal component.
You can eat whatever you want without feeling guilty or losing control.
Learn simple yet effective ways to determine when and how much to eat without needing restrictive rules:

• Understand how your glucose levels are affected by what you eat and the amount of exercise.
• Learn the fundamentals of nutrition in easy-to-understand language.
• Instead of being afraid of blood sugar monitoring, embrace it with curiosity.
• Reduce your anxiety about diabetes self-management.
• Do exercise. It should be a desire rather than an obligation.
• Learn why medications can be a necessary part of your diabetes treatment.

Develop powerful thought patterns to help you live the balanced, energetic life you desire.

STRESS IS YOUR ENEMY!

Diabetes is a very stressful condition to have. It is hard to think about what you eat and make sure you take your medication every day. With stress, the body produces cortisol, which raises blood sugar and makes cells less responsive to insulin. The combination of these factors makes diabetes more difficult to manage. Stress makes you reach for sugary or fatty foods and increases your appetite. Find a stress-relief technique that's right for you. There is a relaxing routine you can try before going to bed. You need to stretch and take a moment to breathe and relax 3-7 times, before sleeping. Walking, meditation and yoga are all effective techniques to relieve stress.
About a quarter of people with diabetes also suffer from depression. Talk to family or friends if you feel overwhelmed. Alternatively, contact experts or diabetic associations in your area to find a support group. Visit a therapist or psychologist for one-on-one assistance. Sleep is also essential. When people

sleep better, they see their stress levels go down. People are encouraged to turn off their phones and stop checking emails or texts two hours before bedtime. The blue light from screens can keep you awake.

STICK TO THE DIET PLAN

Your treatment plan and diet regimen should serve as a roadmap for you. If you stick to your diabetes diet, you'll be less likely to develop problems like heart disease, blindness, or nerve damage. Consult your doctor regularly. Ask your physician what you should do if any part of your treatment is not working well. Finding a healthy balance that helps you control your diabetes and avoid these potential complications is crucial. The best way to get there is to make sure you and your treatment team are in constant communication.

When it comes to weight loss, even small changes in your eating habits can have an impact. Bringing nutritious snacks to work with you can help you avoid the vending machine or plate of cookies that always seem to be tempting you.

For diabetes-friendly snacks, nuts are among the best nutritionally and the most portable options.

KEEP TRACK OF MEALS BY USING A FOOD DIARY

It's easier to follow a diet when you track what you eat by writing down everything you consume. In fact, according to a year-long study published in August 2017 in the Journal of Diabetes Research, people with type 2 diabetes, who consistently wrote down what they ate, lost an average of about 10 pounds over the study period, compared to the control group which lost no weight.

MOVE AND WALK AFTER EVERY MEAL

Also, don't overlook the value of regular exercise. Physical activity has been shown to lower blood pressure, improve heart health, stabilize blood sugar and improve the overall quality of life. According to the authors, prioritizing fitness can help prevent or delay the condition. You know that exercise is important for diabetes management and weight loss, but bear in mind that finding small ways to stay active

throughout the day will also help you burn calories. It's a good idea to start by standing. A 170-pound person can burn about 186 calories standing compared to 139 calories sitting for an hour. Set a timer as a simple reminder to get up and move around, after every 30 minutes. Walking, stretching and crunching, or lifting free weights are all good ways to give your body 30 minutes of rest.

It's all too easy to let the day pass you by without getting some exercise, so add a quick activity at the end of each meal. Take a 10-minute walk after each meal or after all meals. This is critical for blood sugar regulation and weight loss. According to a previous study, people at risk for high blood sugar who walked for 15 minutes after every meal, had better blood sugar management than those who took a 45-minute walk in the morning or afternoon.

AVOID BINGES

If you snack while watching the TV or working on the computer, your efforts to lose weight with diabetes can be thwarted. According to one study, eating in front of a screen with other distractions causes you to more. Eating without distractions causes people to eat less throughout the day. The research also found that paying attention to what you eat can help you maintain a healthy weight without watching calories. Eat every meal at the table and focus on what you're eating.

DON'T DEPRIVE YOURSELF TOO MUCH

The road to good health and weight loss for diabetics is not paved with deprivation. Yes, you should keep track of your calories, but you shouldn't deprive yourself or starve yourself, nor should you eliminate entire food groups, according to Snyder. Make an effort to eat balanced meals and snacks regularly. The need to maintain a healthy balance is imperative. Carbohydrates, proteins, and lipids are all vital in your diet. Ignoring an entire category of foods can lead to an imbalance, which is detrimental. Eating too few calories is also a problem and could indicate an eating disorder. Again, a health expert can help you determine what constitutes a healthy balance of fats, carbohydrates, and proteins in your diet.

MEAL PLANNING HELPS

Meal planning is critical to following any health-oriented diet, let alone a diabetic diet, and only by sticking to a healthy eating pattern can you achieve your goals. The Mediterranean diet, for example, consists primarily of plant-based foods, including vegetables, fruits, whole grains, nuts, beans, and legumes. Some dairy products are allowed, such as cheese and yogurt, while red meat is tolerated in moderation. Instead, fish and poultry are common protein sources in the Mediterranean diet, while olive oil is often the main source of fat.

HEALTHY EATING

Many people assume that excess sugar is why their glucose levels are too high. But they're wrong. While paying attention to how much sugar you eat is essential, it's more important to keep track of your carbohydrates.

Our bodies turn all carbohydrates into sugar for fuel. So while you might think a particular food is fine since it doesn't have much sugar, it could be high in carbohydrates and raise your blood sugar level. We'll discuss carbohydrates in more detail in the next chapter. But for now, just know that a healthy diet that pays attention to carbohydrate levels is one of the best ways to handle type 2 diabetes.

TIPS AND FAQ BEFORE YOU START

A healthy eating pattern for people with diabetes includes healthy choices, favorite foods, dining out, and alcohol in moderation (if desired).

Are you confused about where to start when it comes to grocery shopping or preparing your next meal? I will help you with some simple practice examples before following your 28-day meal plan.

What does a daily meal plan look like?

Here is a general guideline before you work with a registered nutritionist dietician:

Women	Men
30-45 grams of Carbohydrate at each meal, 15 grams Carbohydrate for a snack (based on 1500 cal/day)	45-60 grams of Carbohydrate at each meal, 15-30 grams Carbohydrate for a snack (based on 1800 cal/day)

What should your plate look like?

Aim filling your plate with:
- ¼ plate of Carbohydrate/starchy food
- ¼ plate of Protein food¬
- ½ plate of non-starchy vegetables
- 1 serving (tsp) of fats

Helpful tip:

Try to eat meals and snacks around the same time each day, so your healthcare provider can look for any patterns in blood glucose levels. Checking blood sugar two hours after the start of a meal can let you know how your body responds to the foods you eat. Aim for a blood sugar of less than 140 mg/dL two hours after meals.

NON-STARCHY VEGETABLES [5 grams Carbs / 1 cup serving (raw)]	CARBS FOODS (starches, grains, beans, milk) [All servings below = 15 grams Carbs] *	PROTEIN FOODS [7 grams Protein /once]	FATS [5 grams fat per serving]
Artichoke	½ cup corn	Albacore tuna	2 tbsp avocado
Asparagus	1 cup butternut squash	Beef	1 tsp canola oil
Beets	½ cup parsnips	Chicken breast	6 cashews or almonds
Broccoli	½ cup peas	¼ cup Cottage cheese	1 tbsp chia seeds
Brussel sprouts	½ medium baking potato	1 egg	1 tbsp cream cheese
Cabbage	1 cup cooked pumpkin	Haddock	1 ½ tbsp flax seed
Carrots	½ cup sweet potato	1 tbsp Natural peanut butter	1 tsp margarine
Cauliflower	6 ounces light yogurt	Pork iron	1 tbsp low-fat margarine
Celery		½ cup Ricotta cheese	1 tsp mayonnaise
Cucumber	1 cup low-fat milk	Salmon	1 tsp olive oil
Eggplant	1 cup flavored almond milk	2 Sardines	4 halves pecans/walnuts
Green beans	1 cup soy milk	Seitan	16 pistachios
Greens/lettuce (all kinds)	1 cup buttermilk	Shrimp	2 tbsp low fat salad dressing
Mushroom	¾ cup dry cereal	Sliced deli meat	1 tbsp salad dressing

Okra	½ English muffin	¼ cup tempeh	3 tbsp light sour cream
Onions	1 small wheat tortilla	tofu	2 tbsp sour cream
Pepper	1 small roll of wheat bread	trout	1 tbsp sunflower seeds
Tomato			
Zucchini	1 small wheat pita	Turkey breast	

*Other Carbs food choices:

1 apple (4 oz)	1/3 cup brown ice (cooked)
1 banana (4 oz)	1/3 cup wild rice (cooked)
1 ¼ cup strawberries	½ cup bulgur (cooked)
1 cup cantaloupe	1/3 cup quinoa (cooked)
12 fresh cherries	2 tbsp dry corn meal
17 grapes (3 oz)	1/3 cup whole grain pasta (cooked)
½ mango	1/3 cup hummus
1 mandarin orange	½ cup lentils (cooked)
1 peach	½ cup black beans (cooked)
½ cup kiwi	½ cup kidney beans (cooked)
1 ¼ cup watermelon	½ cup pinto beans (cooked)
½ grapefruit	½ cup split peas (cooked)
¾ cup blueberries	1/3 cup chickpeas (cooked)
1 cup blackberries	1 cup edamame
2 plums	3 cups popcorn (popped)
1 nectarine	½ cup oatmeal (cooked)
1 cup honeydew melon	½ cup fruit cocktail
¾ cup pineapple	6 whole grain crackers

28-DAY MEAL PLAN
WEEK 1

DAYS	BREAKFAST	LUNCH	DINNER
Day 1	Apple Cinnamon Cake	Chicken Arroz	Italian Fish Stew
Day 2	Sweet Onion and Ham Frittata	Pan-Seared Sesame-Crusted Tuna Steaks	Broccoli Quiche (No-Crust)
Day 3	Avocado Toast Breakfast	Pork Chops Pomodoro	Cashew Chicken
Day 4	Blueberry, Citrus and Poppy Muffins	Tilapia Stew with Green Peppers	Salmon With Lemon-Thyme Slices
Day 5	Kale Chips	Mushroom Cutlets with Creamy Sauce	Quick & Easy Beef
Day 6	Zucchini and Yellow Pepper Scramble	Chicken Breast in Red Wine Sauce	Sausage and Pepper Soup
Day 7	Eggs and Mixed Vegetable	Baked Salmon with Garlic Parmesan Topping	Vegan Thai Red Curry

WEEK 2

DAYS	BREAKFAST	LUNCH	DINNER
Day 1	Breakfast Grilled Cheese and Rye	Pan-Seared Sirloin Steak	Beet, Goat Cheese, and Walnut Pesto with Zucchini Noodles
Day 2	English Muffin Melts	Beef and Lentil Soup	Herbed Chicken and Sweet Potato Bake
Day 3	Orange-Honey Yogurt	Balsamic Bean Salsa Salad	Crab Cakes
Day 4	Apple Cinnamon Muffins	Balsamic Chicken and Vegetable Skillet	Basil Meatball Bake
Day 5	Broccoli Purée and Potato Hash Browns	American Sushi Tuna	Zucchini and Tomato Stew
Day 6	Greek Yogurt Sundae	Pan-Seared Sirloin Steak	Chicken Cordon Bleu
Day 7	Apple Cheddar Muffins	Kale and Cauliflower Soup	Shrimp and Halibut Sauté

WEEK 3

DAYS	BREAKFAST	LUNCH	DINNER
Day 1	Choco Chip, Banana and Peanut Butter Cup	Sherry Tofu and Spinach Stir-Fry	Beer Braised Brisket
Day 2	Apple Cinnamon Cake	Citrusy Veg Chicken Roast	Italian Sausage Soup
Day 3	Sweet Onion and Ham Frittata	Oven-Roasted Salmon	Mozzarella and Artichoke Stuffed Spaghetti Squash
Day 4	Avocado Toast Breakfast	BBQ Pork Tacos	Ham and Cheese Stuffed Chicken Breasts
Day 5	Blueberry, Citrus and Poppy Muffins	Chunky Chicken Noodle Soup	Crunchy Lemon Shrimp
Day 6	Kale Chips	Cauliflower Mushroom Risotto	Parmesan-Crusted Pork Chops
Day 7	Zucchini and Yellow Pepper Scramble	Dijon'd Chicken with Rosemary	Mexican Chicken and Rice

WEEK 4

DAYS	BREAKFAST	LUNCH	DINNER
Day 1	Eggs and Mixed Vegetable	Blackened Shrimp	Firenze Pizza
Day 2	Breakfast Grilled Cheese and Rye	Sweet Sherry'd Pork Tenderloin	Chicken Tuscany
Day 3	English Muffin Melts	Green Pepper Skillet Chili	Pistachios and Herb Halibut
Day 4	Orange-Honey Yogurt	Brussels Sprout, Avocado, and Wild Rice Bowl	Sweet Jerk Pork
Day 5	Apple Cinnamon Muffins	Autumn Slaw	Dijon'd Chicken with Rosemary
Day 6	Broccoli Purée and Potato Hash Browns	Lime and Sea Bass Ceviche	Spinach Casserole
Day 7	Greek Yogurt Sundae	Quick & Easy Steak Tacos	Ricotta and Turkey Bell Peppers

BREAKFAST

SCAN ME! RECIPES' COLOR IMAGES

· ·

Prep
10 m

Portion
6 Servings

Cook
50 m

Per Serving
Calories219; fat: 16g; Protein: 9g;
Carbs: 20g

APPLE CINNAMON CAKE (GRAIN-FREE)
· ·

· · · · · · · · · · · · · · · · · · · ·

2 cups almond flour
½ cup Lakanto Monkfruit Sweetener Golden
1½ tsp ground cinnamon
1 tsp baking powder
½ tsp fine sea salt
½ cup plain 2 percent Greek yogurt
2 large eggs
½ tsp pure vanilla extract
1 small apple, chopped into small pieces

Directions

1. Pour 1 cup water into the Instant Pot. Line the base of a 7 by 3-inch round cake pan with parchment paper. Butter the sides of the pan and the parchment or coat with non-stick cooking spray.
2. In a medium bowl, whisk together the almond flour, sweetener, cinnamon, baking powder, and salt. In a smaller bowl, whisk together the yogurt, eggs, and vanilla until no streaks of yolk remain. Add the wet mixture to the dry mixture and stir just until the dry ingredients are evenly moistened, then fold in the apple. The batter will be very thick.
3. Transfer the batter to the prepared pan and, using a rubber spatula, spread it in an even layer. Cover the pan tightly with aluminum foil. Place

the pan on a long-handled silicone steam rack, then, holding the handles of the steam rack, lower it into the Instant Pot. (If you don't have the long-handled rack, use the wire metal steam rack and a homemade sling)
4. Secure the lid and set the Pressure Release to Sealing. Select the Cake, Pressure Cook, or Manual setting and set the cooking time for 40 minutes at high pressure. (The pot will take about 10 minutes to come up to pressure before the cooking program begins.)
5. When the cooking program ends, let the pressure release naturally for 10 minutes, then move the Pressure Release to Venting to release any remaining steam. Open the pot and, wearing heat-resistant mitts, grasp the handles of the steam rack and lift it out of the pot. Uncover the pan, taking care not to get burned by the steam or to drip condensation onto the cake. Let the cake cool in the pan on a cooling rack for about 5 minutes.
6. Run a butter knife around the edge of the pan to loosen the cake from the pan sides. Invert the cake onto the rack, lift off the pan, and peel off the parchment. Let cool for 15 minutes, then invert the cake onto a serving plate. Cut into eight wedges and serve.
Substitution tip: *You can use low-fat yogurt and a pinch of stevia.*

Prep
0 m

Portion
4 Servings

Cook
8 m

Per Serving
110 Calories, 2g fat, 6g Carbs, 17g Protein

SWEET ONION AND HAM OMELET

· ·

4 ounces extra-lean, low-sodium ham slices, chopped
1 cup thinly sliced Vidalia onion
1 1/2 cups egg substitute
1/3 cup shredded, reduced-fat, sharp cheddar cheese

Directions:

1.   Place a medium nonstick skillet over medium-high heat until hot. Coat the skillet with nonstick cooking spray, add ham, and cook until beginning to lightly brown, about 2–3 minutes, stirring frequently. Remove from skillet and set aside on separate plate.
2.   Reduce the heat to medium, coat the skillet with nonstick cooking spray, add onions, and cook 4 minutes or until beginning to turn golden, stirring frequently.
3.   Reduce the heat to medium low, add ham to the onions, and cook 1 minute (this allows the flavors to blend and the skillet to cool slightly before the eggs are added). Pour egg substitute evenly overall, cover, and cook 8 minutes or until puffy and set.
4.   Remove the skillet from the heat, sprinkle cheese evenly overall, cover, and let stand 3 minutes to melt the cheese and develop flavors.
Substitution tip: You can use white onion.

GRILLED CHEESE AND RYE TO START WITH ENERGY

· ·

12 slices rye bread
4 tsp reduced-fat margarine (35% vegetable oil)
2 large eggs
1 1/2 ounces sliced, reduced-fat Swiss cheese, torn in small pieces
Directions:
1.   Spread one side of each bread slice with 1 tsp margarine and set aside.
2.   Place a medium skillet over medium heat until hot. Coat with nonstick cooking spray and add the egg substitute. Cook 1 minute without stirring. Using a rubber spatula, lift up the edges to allow the uncooked portion to run under. Cook 1–2 minutes longer or until eggs are almost set and beginning to puff up slightly. Flip and cook 30 seconds.
3.   Remove the skillet from the heat and spoon half of the eggs on the unbuttered sides of two of the bread slices. Arrange equal amounts of the cheese evenly over each piece.
4.   Return the skillet to medium heat until hot. Coat the skillet with nonstick cooking spray. Add the two sandwiches and cook 3 minutes. If the cheese doesn't melt when frying the sandwich bottom, put it under the broiler until brown. Using a serrated knife, cut each sandwich in half.
Substitution tip: *You can use reduced-fat Mexican blend cheese, or Provolone, Muenster, Mozzarella.*

Prep
5 m

Portion
2 Servings

Cook
7 m

Per Serving
250 Calories, 13g fat, 17g Carbs, 16g Protein

AVOCADO TOAST BREAKFAST

Prep
5 m

Portion
1 Servings

Cook
2 m

Per Serving
Calorie: 250, fat: 8g, Protein:
7g, Carbs: 38g

. . . .

2 slices sprouted grain bread
1–1½ tsp chickpea miso
¼ cup ripe avocado, mashed
Squeeze of lemon juice (about ½ tsp)
A couple pinches of sea salt
1 tsp nutritional yeast (optional)
Freshly ground black pepper to taste
2 thick slices ripe tomato, or a handful of chopped lettuce or baby spinach

Directions

1.   Toast the bread. While it's still warm, spread about ½ tsp of the miso on each slice. Distribute the avocado over the miso and add a squeeze of lemon juice and a pinch of salt. Sprinkle on nutritional yeast (if using), and pepper.

2.   Top with the sliced tomatoes, lettuce, or spinach.

Substitution tip: You can use other mild-flavored miso.

KALE CHIPS

Prep
5 m

Portion
4-6 Servings

Cook
60 m

Per Serving
Per Serving: 60 Calories, 4g fat,
5g Carbs, 3g Protein

. . . .

12 ounces Lacinato kale, stemmed and torn into 3-inch pieces
1 tbsp extra-virgin olive oil
½ tsp kosher salt

Directions:

1.   Adjust oven racks to upper-middle and lower-middle positions and heat oven to 200 degrees. Set wire racks in 2 rimmed baking sheets. Dry kale thoroughly between dish towels, transfer to large bowl, and toss with oil and salt.

2.   Arrange kale on prepared racks, making sure leaves overlap as little as possible. Bake kale until very crisp, 45 to 60 minutes, switching and rotating sheets halfway through baking. Let kale chips cool completely before serving. (Kale chips can be stored in paper towel–lined airtight container for up to 1 day.)

Prep
5 m

Portion
18 Makes

Cook
25 m

Per Serving
Calories165; Carbs: 7g; Protein: 4g;
Fat: 9g

BLUEBERRY, CITRUS AND POPPY MUFFINS

Non-stick cooking spray or paper liners
2 cups whole wheat pastry flour
1 cup almond flour
½ cup Splenda sweetener, granulated
1 tbsp baking powder
2 tsp lemon zest, grated
¾ tsp baking soda
¾ tsp nutmeg, ground
2 tbsp poppy seeds
Pinch of sea salt, ground
2 eggs
1 cup plant-based milk, room temperature
¾ cup plain low-fat yogurt,
½ cup coconut oil, melted
1 tbsp lemon juice
1 tsp vanilla bean extract
1 cup blueberries, frozen or fresh

Directions:

1.   Preheat the oven to 350°F gas mark 4.
2.   Prepare the muffin tin with paper liners or coat with non-stick cooking spray. Set aside.

3.   In a stand mixer, mix the whole wheat pastry flour, almond flour, granulated sweetener, baking powder, lemon zest, baking soda, ground nutmeg, poppy seeds, and ground sea salt.
4.   In a medium-sized plastic jug, mix the eggs, plant-based milk, low-fat yogurt, melted coconut oil, lemon juice, and vanilla bean extract until well combined.
5.   With the mixer on low speed, add the wet ingredients into the dry ingredients until well incorporated.
6.   Gently fold in the blueberries with a rubber spatula.
7.   Use a medium ice cream scoop to evenly spoon the batter into the prepared muffin tin. Bake for 25 minutes or until the toothpick inserted comes out clean.
8.   Place the cooked muffins on a wire rack to cool completely or serve warm with a plant-based butter or organic jam.

Substitution tip: *You can use 1 cup all-purpose flour and 1 cup wholewheat flour in place of the 2 cups whole wheat pastry flour.*

Prep
5 m

Portion
4 Servings

Cook
10 m

Per Serving
Calories196; Carbs: 2g; Protein:
13g; Fat: 11g

ZUCCHINI AND YELLOW PEPPER SPECIAL SCRAMBLE

. . . .

1 tsp olive oil
1 spring onion, diced
½ yellow bell pepper, cut into cubes
½ zucchini, cut into cubes
8 large eggs, beaten
1 tomato, seeded and cut into cubes
2 tsp fresh oregano, diced finely
Salt, ground
Black pepper, ground
Directions:

1. Heat a heavy bottom pan over medium heat and add the olive oil and cook until hot.
2. Toss in the diced spring onion, cubed yellow bell pepper, and the cubed zucchini, fry for 5 minutes until tender.
3. Add the beaten eggs and using a spatula or fork, scramble the egg mixture for 5 minutes or until the eggs are cooked through.
4. Remove the pan off the heat and add the cubed tomato and diced oregano, mix to combine.
5. Season with ground Salt and ground black pepper and serve warm.

Ingredient tip: Smoked Sea salt will add a smoky flavor to the dish.

EGGS AND MIXED VEGETABLE

. . . .

1 broccoli head, cut into florets
1 medium red and green bell peppers, sliced
1 small onion, thinly sliced
¼ cup fresh mixed herbs, roughly chopped
3 tbsp coconut oil, melted and divided
Salt, ground
Black pepper, ground
Paprika spice, ground
8 large eggs
Direction:

1. Heat the oven to 425°F gas mark 7. Line the baking sheet with aluminum foil.
2. In a large bowl, add the broccoli florets, sliced red and green bell peppers, sliced onion, and chopped mixed herbs. Drizzle with 2 tbsp of melted coconut oil and season with ground Salt, ground black pepper, and ground paprika. Toss to combine.
3. Place the baking sheet into the preheated oven and roast the vegetables for 15 to 20 minutes until they are cooked and slightly browned.
4. While the vegetables are cooking, heat a large heavy bottom pan over medium heat and add the remaining 1 tbsp coconut oil until hot.
5. Fry the eggs until they reach your desired consistency.
6. Divide the roast vegetables onto 4 plates and add the fried eggs on top. Serve immediately.

Ingredient tip: Here are some fresh herbs that you can use in this recipe, parsley, basil, thyme, rosemary, spring onion, chives, and sage.

Prep
5 m

Portion
4 Servings

Cook
15-20 m

Per Serving
Calories269; Net Carbs: 8g;
Protein: 14g; Fat: 20g

Prep
5 m

Portion
1 Serving

Cook
0 m

Per Serving
Calories: 238, fat: 11g, Protein: 21g,
Carbs: 16g

BERRIES & GREEK YOGURT SUNDAE

. . . .

1¾ cup plain non-fat Greek yogurt
¼ cup mixed berries (blueberries, strawberries, blackberries)
2 tbsp cashew, walnut, or almond pieces
1 tbsp ground flaxseed
2 fresh mint leaves, shredded

Directions
1. Spoon the yogurt into a small bowl. Top with the berries, nuts, and flaxseed.
2. Garnish with the mint and serve.

Prep
10 m

Portion
12 Makes

Cook
20 m

Per Serving
Calories 162, Carbs 17g, Protein
10g, Fat 5g

GNAMMY APPLE CHEDDAR MUFFINS

. . . .

1 egg
¾ cup tart apple, peel & chop
2/3 cup reduced fat cheddar cheese, grated
2/3 cup skim milk
What you'll need from store cupboard:
2 cup low Carbs baking mix
2 tbsp vegetable oil
1 tsp cinnamon

Directions:
1.   Heat oven to 400 degrees F. Line a 12-cup muffin pan with paper liners.
2.   In a medium bowl, lightly beat the egg. Stir in remaining Ingredients just until moistened. Divide evenly between prepared muffin cups.
3.   Bake 17-20 minutes or until golden brown. Serve warm.
Ingredient tip: You can use extra virgin olive oil.

Prep
7 m

Portion
1 Servings

Cook
0 m

Per Serving
15 Calories, 0g fat 2g Carbs, 1g Protein

ORANGE-HONEY YOGURT

. . . .

Ingredients:
·   *1 cup 2 percent Greek yogurt*
·   *2 tbsp honey*
·   *¼ tsp grated orange zest plus 2 tbsp juice*

Directions:
1.   *Whisk ingredients together in bowl. (Yogurt can be refrigerated for up to 3 days.) Serve.*

BROCCOLI PURÉE AND POTATO HASH BROWNS

. . . .

1 cup broccoli, cut into florets
Sea salt, ground
½ lb. peeled russet potatoes, grated and patted dry
¼ onion, finely chopped
1 tsp olive oil
1 tsp fresh thyme, chopped
Black pepper, ground
Non-stick cooking spray

Directions:
1.   *Put the broccoli florets in a medium-sized pot and add a pinch of ground sea salt. Boil for 2 to 3 minutes until tender.*
2.   *Allow it to drain completely, making sure all excess water is gone. Transfer into a food processor*

and purée. Set aside.
3.   *Place the grated potatoes, finely chopped onion, olive oil, and chopped fresh thyme in a large bowl. Season with ground sea salt and ground black pepper and mix.*
4.   *Place a large heavy bottom pan over medium heat and spray with non-stick cooking spray.*
5.   *Add a ¼ cup of the potato mixture per hash brown, press down with a spatula, and cook for 5 to 7 minutes until the bottom is firm and golden. Flip the hash brown over and cook for 5 more minutes until completely cooked through and golden.*
6.   *Remove and repeat with the remaining potato mixture.*
7.   *Serve it with the homemade broccoli purée.*
Ingredient tip: You can use unsweetened applesauce in place of the broccoli purée.

Prep
10 m

Portion
4 Servings

Cook
25 m

Per Serving
Calories106; Carbs: 18g; Protein: 1g; Fat: 3g

Prep
5 m

Portion
1 Serving

Cook
0 m

Per Serving
315; Protein: 15g; Carbs: 18g; Fat: 25g

CHOCO CHIP, BANANA AND PEANUT BUTTER CUP

½ cup low-fat yogurt, plain
Pinch of Stevia sweetener
2 tbsp organic peanut butter, smooth
1 tbsp dark chocolate chips
Pinch of sea salt, ground
1 tbsp salted peanuts, roughly chopped
½ banana, chopped

Direction:
1.   In a dessert bowl, combine the low-fat yogurt and a pinch of stevia.
2.   Add the organic peanut butter, dark chocolate chips, and the chopped banana and mix to combine.
3.   Sprinkle with a pinch of ground sea salt and the roughly chopped peanuts.
Ingredient tip: Use 55% dark chocolate if you do not want a bitter cocoa flavor.

ENGLISH MUFFIN MELTS

. . . .

4 whole-wheat English muffins, cut in half
2 tbsp reduced-fat mayonnaise
3 ounces sliced reduced-fat Swiss cheese, torn in small pieces
4 ounces oven-roasted deli turkey, finely chopped

Directions:
1. Preheat the broiler.
2. Arrange the muffin halves on a baking sheet and place under the broiler for 1–2 minutes or until lightly toasted. Remove from broiler and spread 3/4 tsp mayonnaise over each muffin half.
3. Arrange the cheese pieces evenly on each muffin half and top with the turkey.
4. Return to the broiler and cook 3 minutes, or until the turkey is just beginning to turn golden and the cheese has melted.

Substitution tip: *You can use reduced-fat Mexican blend cheese, or Provolone, Muenster, Mozzarella.*

Prep
5 m

Portion
8 Makes

Cook
3 m

Per Serving
120 Calories, 3g fat, 15g Carbs, 9g Protein

APPLE CINNAMON MUFFINS

. . . .

1 cup apple, diced fine
2/3 cup skim milk
¼ cup reduced-calorie margarine, melted
1 egg, lightly beaten
What you'll need from the store cupboard
1 2/3 cups flour
1 tbsp Stevia
2 ½ tsp baking powder
1 tsp cinnamon
½ tsp sea salt
¼ tsp nutmeg

Non-stick cooking spray

Directions:
1. Heat oven to 400 degrees F. Spray a 12-cup muffin pan with cooking spray.
2. In a large bowl, combine dry Ingredients and stir to mix.
3. In another bowl, beat milk, margarine, and egg to combine.
4. Pour wet Ingredients into dry Ingredients and stir just until moistened. Gently fold in apples.
5. Spoon into prepared muffin pan. Bake 25 minutes, or until tops are lightly browned.

Ingredient tip: *You can use pears in place of apples.*

Prep
15 m

Portion
15 Makes

Cook
25 m

Per Serving
Calories 119, Carbs 17g, Protein 3g, Fat 4g

SIDES & SALADS

SCAN ME! RECIPES' COLOR IMAGES

Prep
5 m

Portion
1 Serving

Cook
5 m

Per Serving
Calories 356;,Carbs 10g 5g ,Protein
25g Fat 25g

ASPARAGUS AND BACON SALAD

. . . .

1 hard-boiled egg, peeled and sliced
1 2/3 cups asparagus, chopped
2 slices bacon, cooked crisp and crumbled
What you'll need from store cupboard:
1 tsp extra virgin olive oil
1 tsp red wine vinegar
½ tsp Dijon mustard
Pinch salt and pepper, to taste

Directions:
1.   Bring a pot of water to a boil. Add the asparagus and cook 2-3 minutes or until tender-crisp. Drain and add cold water to stop the cooking process.
2.   In a small bowl, whisk together, mustard, oil, vinegar, and salt and pepper to taste.
3.   Place the asparagus on a plate, top with egg and bacon. Drizzle with vinaigrette and serve.
Substitution tip: you can replace Dijon mustard with low-fat mayonnaise.

Prep
15 m

Portion
4 Serving

Cook
0 m

Per Serving
Calories: 489; Protein: 7g; Carbs:
14g; Fat: 45g

MIXED GREENS AND PUMPKIN SEED SALAD

. . . .

FOR THE DRESSING:
½ cup olive oil
¼ cup lemon juice, freshly squeezed
1 tsp garlic, minced
Sea salt, ground
Black pepper, ground
FOR THE SALAD:
10 oz leafy greens, salad mix
2 avocados, chopped
1 cup cucumber, chopped
1 cup carrots, grated
1 cup celery, diced

½ cup pumpkin seeds, toasted
Directions:
FOR THE DRESSING:
1.   In a small jug, mix the olive oil, fresh lemon juice, and minced garlic. Season with salt and pepper.
FOR THE SALAD:
1.   In a large serving bowl, add the mixed leafy greens, chopped avocados, chopped cucumber, grated carrots, diced celery, and toasted pumpkin seeds.
2.   Drizzle the homemade dressing and toss to combine.
3.   Serve or refrigerate for later.
Substitution tip: You can use green bell pepper in place of the celery.

Type 2 Diabetes Cookbook

Prep
10 m

Portion
6 Servings

Cook
25-30 m

Per Serving
Calorie: 87, fat: 5g, Protein: 5g,
Carbs: 7g

CHEESY CAULI BAKE

. . . .

3 tbsp tahini
2 tbsp nutritional yeast
1 tbsp lemon juice
½ tsp pure maple syrup
½ tsp sea salt
½ cup + 1 tbsp plain non-dairy milk
3–3½ cups cauliflower florets, cut or broken in small pieces
Topping
1 tbsp almond meal or breadcrumbs
½ tbsp nutritional yeast
Pinch sea salt

Directions:

1. Preheat the oven to 425°F. Use cooking spray to lightly coat the bottom and sides of an 8" x 8" (or similar size) baking dish.
2. In a small bowl, whisk together the tahini, nutritional yeast, lemon juice, maple syrup or agave nectar, and salt. Gradually whisk in the milk until it all comes together smoothly. In the baking dish, add the cauliflower and pour in the sauce, stir thoroughly to coat the cauliflower. Cover with foil and bake for 25 to 30 minutes, stirring only once, until the cauliflower is tender.
3. In a small bowl, toss together the topping ingredients. Remove the foil from the cauliflower, and sprinkle on the topping. Return to the oven and set oven to broil. Allow to cook for a minute or so until the topping is golden brown. Remove, let sit for a few minutes, then serve.

Ingredient tip: You can use agave nectar in place of maple syrup.

PAN-ROASTED BROCCOLI

. . . .

¼ tsp salt
⅛ tsp pepper
2 tbsp extra-virgin olive oil
1¾ pounds broccoli, florets cut into 1½-inch pieces, stalks peeled and cut on bias into ¼-inch-thick slices

Directions:

1.   Stir 3 tbsp water, salt, and pepper together in small bowl until salt dissolves; set aside. Heat oil in 12-inch nonstick skillet over medium-high heat until just smoking. Add broccoli stalks in even layer and cook, without stirring, until browned on bottoms, about 2 minutes. Add florets to skillet and toss to combine. Cook, without stirring, until bottoms of florets just begin to brown, 1 to 2 minutes.
2.   Add water mixture and cover skillet. Cook until broccoli is bright green but still crisp, about 2 minutes. Uncover and continue to cook until water has evaporated, broccoli stalks are tender, and florets are crisp-tender, about 2 minutes. Serve.

Ingredient tip: You can replace broccoli with zucchini.

Prep
5 m

Portion
6 Servings

Cook
10 m

Per Serving
70 Calories, 5g fat, 5g Carbs, 2g Protein

Prep
5 m

Portion
4 Servings

Cook
21 m

Per Serving
50 Calories, 0g fat., 12g Carbs, 2g
Protein

SAUCY EGGPLANT AND CAPERS

. . . .

10 ounces eggplant, diced (about 2 1/2 cups)
1 (14.5-ounce) can stewed tomatoes with Italian seasonings
2 tbsp chopped fresh basil
2 tsp capers, drained
2 tsp extra virgin olive oil (optional)

Directions:
1.   Bring the eggplant and tomatoes to boil in a large saucepan over high heat. Reduce the heat, *cover tightly, and simmer 20 minutes or until the eggplant is very tender.*
2.   Remove the saucepan from the heat, stir in the basil, capers, and 2 tsp extra virgin olive oil (if desired), and let stand 3 minutes to develop flavors.

Prep
10 m

Portion
4 Servings

Cook
0 m

Per Serving
Calories: 269; Protein: 3g; Carbs:
23g; Fat: 21g

SPICY GRAPEFRUIT AND AVOCADO SALAD

. . . .

1 head lettuce, torn into small pieces
2 ripe avocados, pitted and cubed
2 grapefruits, peeled and cut into wedges
1 tsp grapefruit zest
2 tbsp olive oil
¼ tsp red pepper flakes
Sea salt

Directions:
1. Place the torn lettuce leaves onto a serving platter.
2. Scatter the cubed avocado and peeled grapefruit wedges.
3. Sprinkle the grapefruit zest over the salad.
4. Drizzle with olive oil and season with red pepper flakes and sea salt.
Ingredient tip: if you are assuming hypertension drugs replace grapefruits with oranges.

Prep
5 m

Portion
4 Servings

Cook
25 m

Per Serving
160 Calories, 12g fat, 9g Carbs, 3g
Protein

BRAISED FENNEL WITH WHITE WINE AND PARMESAN

. . . .

3 tbsp extra-virgin olive oil
2 fennel bulbs, stalks discarded, bulbs cut vertically into ½-inch-thick slices
Salt and pepper
⅓ cup dry white wine
¼ cup grated Parmesan cheese

Directions:
1. Heat 2 tbsp oil in 12-inch non-stick skillet over medium heat until shimmering. Add fennel and sprinkle with ⅛ tsp salt and ⅛ tsp pepper. Add wine, cover, and simmer for 15 minutes.
2. Turn slices over and continue to simmer, covered, until fennel is nearly tender, has absorbed most of liquid, and starts to turn golden, about 10 minutes.
3. Turn fennel again and continue to cook until golden on second side, about 4 minutes. Transfer to serving platter, drizzle with remaining 1 tbsp oil, and sprinkle with Parmesan. Serve.

Prep
5 m

Portion
6 Servings

Cook
10 m

Per Serving
70 Calories, 5g fat, 5g Carbs, 2g
Protein

CAPRESE SALAD

. . . .

3 medium tomatoes, cut into 8 slices
2 (1-oz.) slices mozzarella cheese, cut into strips
¼ cup fresh basil, sliced thin
What you'll need from store cupboard:
2 tsp extra-virgin olive oil
1/8 tsp salt
Pinch black pepper

Directions:
1. Place tomatoes and cheese on serving plates. Sprinkle with salt and pepper. Drizzle oil over and top with basil. Serve.

Prep
5 m

Portion
4 Servings

Cook
15 m

Per Serving
Calories: 499; Protein: 11g; Carbs: 8g; Fat: 47g

PARMESAN AND ZUCCHINI FRITTERS

. . . .

4 cups zucchini, julienned
2 tsp sea salt, ground
½ cup whole wheat flour
2 large eggs
½ cup parmesan cheese, grated
12 tbsp mayonnaise, remove 2 tbsp into a bowl
6 tsp minced garlic, divided
2 tbsp extra-virgin olive oil
1 tbsp lemon juice
½ tsp lemon zest
Black pepper, ground

Directions:

1.   Place a colander over a large bowl and put in the julienned zucchini. Sprinkle with ground sea salt, mix well, and let them stand for 10 minutes until the liquid drains. Gently squeeze the julienned zucchini to remove any extra liquid.
2.   In a large bowl, add the julienned zucchini, whole wheat flour, eggs, grated vegan parmesan cheese, 2 tbsp mayonnaise, half of the minced garlic, and mix well.
3.   Place paper towels on a large plate to absorb the oil from the fritters.
4.   Heat the olive oil in a heavy bottom pan over medium-high heat. Drop the zucchini mixture into the pan, one spoonful at a time, and press down with a spatula to form a patty.
5.   Cook the fritters for 3 minutes on each side, until lightly browned. Place the cooked fritters onto the prepared plate with the paper towels to drain.
6.   In a small bowl, add the remaining mayonnaise, minced garlic, lemon zest, lemon juice, and mix well to make a dipping sauce. Season with ground sea salt and ground black pepper.
7.   Serve the fritters warm with the dipping sauce on the side.

Substitution tip: *you can use a non-vegan parmesan cheese for this recipe, or sharp cheddar cheese.*

SKILLET-ROASTED VEGGIES

. . . .

5 ounces asparagus spears, trimmed and cut into 2-inch pieces (1 cup total), patted dry
3 ounces sliced portobello mushrooms (1/2 of a 6-ounce package)
1/2 medium red bell pepper, cut in thin strips
1/4 tsp salt
1/8 tsp black pepper

Directions:

1.   Place a large nonstick skillet over medium-high heat until hot. Coat the skillet with nonstick cooking spray and add the asparagus, mushrooms, and bell pepper. Coat the vegetables with nonstick cooking spray and sprinkle evenly with the salt and black pepper.
2.   Cook 5–6 minutes, or until the vegetables begin to richly brown on the edges. Use two utensils to stir as you would when stir-frying.
3.   Remove from the heat, cover tightly, and let stand 2 minutes to develop flavors.

Substitution tip: *portobello mushrooms can be substituted with zucchini.*

Prep
5 m

Portion
4 Servings

Cook
6 m

Per Serving
15 Calories, 0g fat, 3g Carbs, 1g Protein

TUNA, GREEN BEAN AND EGG SALAD

• •

3 oz green beans, washed and trimmed
3 large eggs
3 oz fresh tuna fillets, rinsed and dried
4 tbsp extra virgin olive oil, divided
Sea salt, ground
Black pepper, ground
3 cups mixed lettuce leaves
1 cup cherry tomatoes, washed and halved
1 cup marinated artichoke hearts, quartered and drained
½ cup black olives, pitted
½ lemon, juiced

Direction:

1. In a large pot, add water and salt and bring it to a boil and fill a separate bowl with ice water.
2. Place the trimmed green beans into the boiling water and cook for 3 minutes, or until bright green and tender. Using a slotted spoon transfer the cooked green beans into the ice water bowl briefly.
3. With the pot of water already at a gentle boil, add the eggs. Cook for 10 minutes, then transfer into the ice water bath.
4. Heat a large heavy bottom pan on medium-high heat until hot.
5. Coat the dried tuna fillets with 1 tbsp of olive oil, and season generously with salt and pepper.
6. Place the tuna fillet in the hot pan, and sear for 2 minutes on each side for medium-rare. The fish will still be deep pink in the center.
7. Put the tuna fillet onto a cutting board and cut it into thick pieces.
8. Peel the cooked eggs and slice them into quarters.
9. When ready to serve, divide the mixed lettuce, quartered eggs, tuna fillet, halved cherry tomatoes, drained and quartered artichoke hearts, pitted olives, and cooked green beans among 4 serving dishes. Finish off by drizzling with the remaining 3 tbsp of olive oil and lemon juice.

Substitution tip: You can replace the artichoke hearts with steamed asparagus or brussels sprouts. Ingredient tip: you can use a mix of green and black olives.

Prep
5 m

Portion
6 Servings

Cook
20 m

Per Serving
Calories: 431; Protein: 28g; Carbs: 15g; Fat: 30g

AUTUMN SLAW

• • • • • • • • • • • • • • • • • •

10 cup cabbage, shredded
½ red onion, diced fine
¾ cup fresh Italian parsley, chopped
What you'll need from store cupboard:
¾ cup almonds, slice & toasted
¾ cup dried cranberries
1/3 cup vegetable oil
¼ cup apple cider vinegar
2 tbsp. sugar free maple syrup
4 tsp Dijon mustard
½ tsp salt
Salt & pepper, to taste

Directions:

1. In a large bowl, whisk together vinegar, oil, syrup, Dijon, and ½ tsp salt. Add the onion and stir to combine. Let rest 10 minutes, or cover and refrigerate until ready to use.
2. After 10 minutes, add remaining Ingredients to the dressing mixture and toss to coat. Taste and season with salt and pepper if needed. Cover and chill 2 hours before serving.

Substitution tip: you can replace Dijon mustard with low-fat mayonnaise. You can use agave nectar in place of maple syrup.

Prep
15 m

Portion
8 Servings

Chill Time
2 h

Per Serving
Calories 133, Carbs 12g, Protein 2g, Fat 9g

Prep
5 m

Portion
4 Servings

Cook
11 m

Per Serving
35 Calories, 2g fat, 5g Carbs, 1g
Protein

ROASTED BEANS AND GREEN ONIONS

· · · · · · · · · ·

8 ounces green string beans, trimmed
4 whole green onions, trimmed and cut in fourths
(about 3-inch pieces)
1 1/2 tsp extra virgin olive oil
1/4 tsp salt

Directions:
1.   Preheat the oven to 425°F.
2.   Line a baking sheet with foil and coat the foil with nonstick cooking spray.
3.   Toss the beans, onions, and oil together in a medium bowl. Arrange them in a thin layer on the baking sheet.
4.   Bake for 8 minutes and stir gently, using two utensils as you would for a stir-fry. Bake another 3–4 minutes or until the beans begin to brown on the edges and are tender-crisp.
5.   Remove the pan from the oven and sprinkle the beans with salt.

ENDIVE AND SWEET POTATO BAKE

· ·

Non-stick cooking spray
2 endives, leaves separated and divided
2 orange sweet potatoes, peeled and thinly sliced
Black pepper, ground
1 tbsp fennel seeds, ground
½ tsp cinnamon, ground
¼ tsp nutmeg, ground
1 cup vegetable broth

Directions:
1.   Heat the oven to 375°F gas mark 5. Prepare a deep baking dish by coating it with non-stick cooking spray.
2.   Cover the bottom of the baking dish with half the endive leaves and layer half the thinly sliced sweet potatoes on top.
3.   Sprinkle the ground black pepper, ground fennel seeds, and half the ground cinnamon and ground nutmeg on top of the potatoes.
4.   Continue to do this for the next few layers, until all the endive leaves, sliced sweet potatoes, ground cinnamon, ground fennel seeds, and ground nutmeg is used.
5.   Add the vegetable broth and cover the deep baking dish with aluminum foil.
6.   Bake for 45 minutes until the vegetables are tender.
7.   Serve hot.
Substitution tip: You can use white sweet potatoes or yams for this recipe, and you can replace the endives with 1 fennel bulb sliced.

Prep
5 m

Portion
4 Servings

Cook
45 m

Per Serving
Calories: 153; Protein: 3g; Carbs: 33g;
Fat: 2g

POULTRY

SCAN ME! RECIPES' COLOR IMAGES

Prep
10 m

Portion
4

Cook
25 m

Per Serving
Calories 161, Carbs 13g, Protein
14g, Fat 5g

CHICKEN ARROZ

1 onion, diced
1 red pepper, diced
2 cup chicken breast, cooked and cubed
1 cup cauliflower, grated
1 cup peas, thaw
2 tbsp. cilantro, diced
½ tsp lemon zest
What you'll need from store cupboard:
14 ½ oz. low sodium chicken broth
¼ cup black olives, sliced
¼ cup sherry
1 clove garlic, diced
2 tsp extra virgin olive oil
¼ tsp salt
¼ tsp cayenne pepper

Directions:

1.   Heat oil in a large skillet over med-high heat. Add pepper, onion and garlic and cook 1 minute. Add the cauliflower and cook, stirring frequently, until light brown, 4-5 minutes.

2.   Stir in broth, sherry, zest and seasonings. Bring to a boil. Reduce heat, cover and simmer 15 minutes.

3.   Stir in the chicken, peas and olives. Cover and simmer another 3-6 minutes or until heated through. Serve garnished with cilantro.

Ingredient tip: *to get the best of this recipe use a mix of green and black olives.*

Prep
5 m

Portion
2

Cook
15 m

Per Serving
Calories: 377; Protein: 47g; Carbs: 8g; Fat: 16g

CHICKEN BREAST IN RED WINE SAUCE

4 chicken breasts, skinless and boneless
1 tbsp avocado oil
Salt, ground
Black pepper, ground
2 medium zucchini, cut into bite-size pieces
1 tsp fresh thyme
¼ cup dry red wine

Directions:

1.   Butterfly the chicken breasts and pat dry with paper towels. Season with ground Salt and ground black pepper.
2.   In a heavy bottom pan on medium heat, add the avocado oil until hot.
3.   Gently place the chicken breasts into the hot pan, and fry for 4 to 5 minutes, then turn the chicken breasts over and cook for another 4 minutes.
4.   Place the chicken breasts onto a cutting board to rest.
5.   In the same pan, add the bite-size zucchini and fresh thyme, and fry for 2 to 3 minutes, until browned and al dente.
6.   Portion the zucchini between 2 serving plates and place the chicken breasts on top.
7.   Add the dry red wine into the same pan, and simmer gently for 2 minutes, until reduced by half. Use a wooden spoon to scrape any browned bits from the bottom of the pan.
8.   Pour the dry red wine reduction over the chicken breasts and zucchini.

Substitution tip: you can replace avocado oil with extra virgin oil.

Prep
10 m

Portion
4

Cook
20 m

Per Serving
Calories 386, Carbs 11g, Protein
43g, Fat 18g

BALSAMIC CHICKEN AND VEGETABLE SKILLET

1 lb. chicken breasts, cut in 1-inch cubes
1 cup cherry tomatoes, halved
1 cup broccoli florets
1 cup baby Bella mushrooms, sliced
1 tbsp. fresh basil, diced
What you'll need from store cupboard:
1/2 recipe homemade pasta, cooked and drain well
½ cup low sodium chicken broth
3 tbsp. balsamic vinegar
2 tbsp extra-virgin olive oil, divided
1 tsp pepper
½ tsp garlic powder
½ tsp salt
½ tsp red pepper flakes

Directions:

1.   Heat oil in a large, deep skillet over med-high heat. Add chicken and cook until browned on all sides, 8-10 minutes.

2.   Add vegetables, basil, broth, and seasonings. Cover, reduce heat to medium and cook 5 minutes, or vegetables are tender.

3.   Uncover and stir in cooked pasta and vinegar. Cook until heated through, 3-4 minutes. Serve.

Ingredient tip: you can replace pasta with rice (Jasmine rice possibly).

Prep
10 m

Portion
4

Cook
2 h

Per Serving
Calories: 543; Protein: 42g; Carbs:
21g; Fat: 32g

CITRUSY VEG CHICKEN ROAST

2 tbsp rosemary, thyme, and oregano, stems
removed
1 orange, zested, and cut into quarters
12 garlic cloves, peeled and divided
3 tbsp extra-virgin olive oil, extra for drizzling
3 tbsp plant-based butter
2 tsp Salt, ground and divided
2½ tsp black pepper, ground and divided
2 medium cauliflower heads, cut into florets
12 oz carrots, peeled and thickly sliced
1 (6 – 7 lb.) whole chicken

Directions:

1.   Preheat the oven to 400°F gas mark 6. Place a
deep roasting pan to the side.
2.   In a food chopper, add the rosemary, thyme,
oregano, orange zest, 4 garlic cloves, olive oil, plant-
based butter, 1 tsp ground Salt, and ½ tsp ground

black pepper, process until minced. Scoop out 1 tbsp
of the mixture and set aside.
3.   Place the cauliflower florets, thickly sliced
carrots, and 4 garlic cloves in the deep roasting pan.
Season with ½ tsp ground Salt and ½ tsp ground
black pepper and drizzle with olive oil. Place the
whole chicken on top of the vegetables, making sure
to place the chicken breast side up.
4.   Gently loosen the skin of the chicken with your
fingers and rub the herb mixture under the skin.
Season the outside of the whole chicken with the
remaining ground Salt and ground black pepper.
Insert the orange quarters, 1 tbsp reserved herb
mixture, and the remaining garlic cloves inside the
chicken cavity.
5.   Roast for 1½ to 2 hours, until fully cooked.
Substitution tip: You can use a lemon in place of the
orange.

Prep
5 m

Portion
4

Cook
13 m

Per Serving
160 Calories, 6g fat., 1g Carbs, 24g
Protein

DIJON'D CHICKEN WITH ROSEMARY

1 tbsp Dijon mustard
1 tbsp extra virgin olive oil
1/4 tsp dried rosemary
4 (4-ounce) boneless, skinless chicken breasts, rinsed and patted dry

Directions:
1.   Using a fork, stir the mustard, olive oil, and rosemary together in a small bowl until well blended and set aside.
2.   Place a medium nonstick skillet over medium heat until hot. Coat the skillet with nonstick cooking spray, add the chicken, and cook 5 minutes.
3.   Turn the chicken, then spoon equal amounts of the mustard mixture over each piece. Reduce the heat to medium low, cover tightly, and cook 7 minutes or until the chicken is no longer pink in the center.
4.   Turn the chicken several times to blend the mustard mixture with the pan drippings, place the chicken on a serving platter, and spoon the mustard mixture over all.

Prep
20 m

Portion
4

Cook
25 m

Per Serving
Calories: 251; Protein: 24g; Carbs:
11g; Fat: 12g

CHICKEN CORDON BLEU

4 chicken breast halves, boneless and skinless
4 slices ham
1 cup mozzarella cheese, grated
½ cup skim milk
½ cup fat free sour cream
What you'll need from store cupboard:
½ can low fat condensed cream of chicken soup
½ cup corn flakes, crushed
½ tsp lemon juice
¼ tsp paprika
½ tsp pepper
½ tsp garlic powder
¼ tsp salt
Non-stick cooking spray

Directions:

1.   Heat oven to 350 degrees. Spray a 13x9-inch baking dish with cooking spray.

2.   Flatten chicken to ¼-inch thick. Sprinkle with pepper and top with slice of ham and 3 tbsp of cheese down the middle. Roll up, tuck ends under and secure with a toothpick.

3.   Pour milk into a shallow bowl. In a separate shallow bowl, combine corn flakes and seasonings. Dip chicken in milk then roll in corn flake mixture and place in prepared dish.

4.   Bake 25-30 minutes or until chicken is cooked through.

5.   In a small saucepan, whisk together soup, sour cream, and lemon juice until combined. Cook over medium heat until hot.

6.   Remove toothpicks from chicken and place on plates, top with sauce and serve.

Light version: remove low fat condensed cream of chicken soup from ingredients.

Prep
10 m

Portion
4

Cook
20 m

Per Serving
Calories: 432; 4g; Protein: 43g;
Carbs: 6g; Fat: 26g

HAM AND CHEESE STUFFED CHICKEN BREASTS

4 chicken breasts, deboned and skinless
4 slices cold meats
4 slices cheddar cheese
1 large egg, beaten
1 cup almond flour
1 tsp Salt, ground
1 tsp black pepper, ground
2 tbsp coconut oil

Directions:
1. Butterfly the chicken breasts in half horizontally. One side should remain attached.
2. Place 1 slice of cold meat and 1 slice of cheddar cheese on one side of the chicken breasts, close them and secure with wooden toothpicks.
3. In a shallow mixing bowl, add the almond flour, ground Salt and ground black pepper, and mix.

4. Dip the stuffed chicken breasts one at a time into the beaten egg and let it drip, then into the seasoned almond flour.
5. Heat the coconut oil in a large heavy bottom pan over medium-high heat until hot.
6. Gently place in the stuffed chicken breasts, and fry for 8 minutes on each side, until cooked through and the cheese has melted.

Substitution tip: You can use Swiss cheese or blue cheese in place of the cheddar cheese.

Type 2 Diabetes Cookbook

Prep
10 m

Portion
4

Cook
10 m

Per Serving
Calories 483, Carbs 19g, Protein 33g Fat 32g

CASHEW CHICKEN

. . . .

1 lb. skinless boneless chicken breast, cut in cubes
1/2 onion, sliced
2 tbsp. green onion, diced
½ tsp fresh ginger, peeled and grated
What you'll need from store cupboard:
1 cup whole blanched cashews, toasted
1 clove garlic, diced fine
4 tbsp. oil
2 tbsp. dark soy sauce
2 tbsp. hoisin sauce
2 tbsp. water
2 tsp corn-starch
2 tsp dry sherry
1 tsp Stevia
1 tsp sesame seed oil

Directions:
1. *Place chicken in a large bowl and add corn-starch, sherry, and ginger. Stir until well mixed.*
2. *In a small bowl, whisk together soy sauce, hoisin, Splenda, and water stirring until smooth.*
3. *Heat the oil in a wok or a large skillet over high heat. Add garlic and onion and cook, stirring until garlic sizzles, about 30 seconds.*
4. *Stir in chicken and cook, stirring frequently, until chicken is almost done, about 2 minutes.*
5. *Reduce heat to medium and stir in sauce mixture. Continue cooking and stirring until everything is blended together. Add cashews and cook 30 seconds.*
6. *Drizzle with sesame oil, and cook another 30 seconds, stirring constantly. Serve immediately garnished with green onions.*

Substitution tip: *you can replace sesame seed oil with peanut oil.*

Prep
5 m

Portion
4

Cook
20 m

Per Serving
Calories: 251; Protein: 24g; Carbs: 11g; Fat: 12g

HERBED CHICKEN AND SWEET POTATO BAKE

2 tbsp coconut oil
1 medium onion, sliced
2 medium white sweet potatoes, cut into chunks
1 lb. cherry tomatoes, halved
3 tsp garlic, crushed
¼ cup dry white wine
4 chicken thighs, deboned and skinless
1 tsp mixed herbs
Sea salt, ground
Black pepper, ground
½ basil, chopped

Directions:
1. Preheat the oven to 400°F gas mark 6. Place a deep baking dish to one side.
2. Heat the olive oil in a large heavy bottom pan over medium-high heat until hot.

3. Add the thinly sliced onion, and fry for 2 to 3 minutes, until softened.
4. Add the sweet potato chunks and fry for 1 to 2 minutes, until browned.
5. Mix in the halved cherry tomatoes, crushed garlic, the dry white wine, and mix until incorporated.
6. Season the deboned chicken thighs with mixed herbs, ground sea salt, and ground black pepper.
7. Transfer the vegetable mixture into the deep baking dish and add the chicken thighs onto the vegetables, then place the baking dish into the oven.
8. Roast for 15 minutes, until the chicken thighs are fully cooked and the vegetables are gently browned.
9. Garnish with chopped basil and serve hot.

Prep	**Portion**	**Cook**	**Per Serving**
10 m	4	15 m	Calories 462, Carbs 6g, Protein 55g, Fat 23g

CHICKEN TUSCANY

. . . .

1½ lbs. chicken breasts, boneless, skinless and sliced thin
1 cup zucchini, chopped
1 cup half-n-half
What you'll need from store cupboard:
½ cup reduced fat parmesan cheese
½ cup low sodium chicken broth
½ cup sun dried tomatoes
2 tbsp extra-virgin olive oil
1 tsp Italian seasoning
1 tsp garlic powder

Directions:
1.   Heat oil in a large skillet over med-high heat. Add chicken and cook 3-5 minutes per side, or until browned and cooked through. Transfer to a plate.
2.   Add half-n-half, broth, cheese and seasonings to the pan. Whisk constantly until sauce starts to thicken. Add zucchini and tomatoes and cook, stirring frequently, until zucchini starts to wilt, about 2-3 minutes.
3.   Add chicken back to the pan and cook just long enough to heat through.

Ingredient tip: If you don't have half-and-half, do as I did and just pour equal parts milk and cream into a jar, shake it a bit (unlike cream, it will never turn into whipped cream or butter, no matter how hard you shake it!) and put it in the fridge.

Prep
10 m

Portion
4

Cook
50 m

Per Serving
Calories: 280; Protein: 24g; Carbs: 14g; Fat: 14g

RICOTTA AND TURKEY BELL PEPPERS

· ·

Non-stick cooking spray
1 tsp extra-virgin olive oil
1 lb. turkey breast, ground
½ red onion, finely chopped
1 tsp garlic, crushed
1 tomato, finely chopped
2 medium carrots, peeled and cut into small cubes
¼ cup peas, thawed
½ tsp basil, finely chopped
Salt
Black pepper, ground
4 medium red bell peppers, tops cut off, seeds removed
2 oz ricotta cheese, crumbled
¼ cup water

Directions:

1.   Heat the oven to 350°F or gas mark 4. Use non-stick cooking spray to coat a baking dish and set it aside.
2.   In a heavy bottom pan, heat the 1 tsp olive oil until hot.
3.   Add the ground turkey into the pan and cook for 6 minutes using a fork to break up the ground turkey until it is browned.
4.   Add and fry the finely chopped onion, cubed carrots, thawed peas, and crushed garlic for 3 minutes until softened.
5.   Stir in the finely chopped tomato and chopped basil. Season with ground Salt and ground black pepper.
6.   Place the red bell peppers cut side up in the baking dish. Spoon the filling equally into the 4 bell pepper.
7.   Sprinkle the crumbled ricotta cheese on top of the filling.
8.   Gently add ¼ cup of water into the baking dish and cover with aluminum foil.
9.   Bake for 40 minutes until the peppers are soft.

Substitution tip: *You can use chicken breasts in place of the turkey breasts. You can use feta cheese instead of ricotta cheese.*

Prep	**Portion**	**Cook**	**Per Serving**
5 m	4	20 m	Calories 457, Carbs 20g, Protein 33g Fat 27g

CRISPY ITALIAN CHICKEN WITH ZUCCHINI

· ·

4 thin chicken breasts, boneless and skinless
2 medium zucchinis, sliced
3 tbsp. margarine, divided
What you'll need from store cupboard:
½ cup Italian breadcrumbs
½ cup + 1 tbsp. reduced fat parmesan, grated
¼ cup flour
2 cloves garlic, diced fine

Directions:

1.   Melt 4 tbsp margarine in a shallow glass dish in the microwave. In another shallow dish, combine breadcrumbs, flour, and ½ cup parmesan.
2.   Melt 2 tbsp margarine in a large skillet over medium heat. Dip chicken in the melted butter, then breadcrumbs to coat and add to skillet. Cook 3-4 minutes per side until crispy and chicken is cooked through. Transfer to paper towel lined plate.
3.   Add remaining 2 tbsp butter to the skillet and when melted add garlic. Cook 1 minute. Add zucchini and cook, stirring occasionally, until tender, about 5-8 minutes.
4.   Salt and pepper to taste and add 1 tbsp parmesan. Add chicken back to skillet just to heat through. Serve.

Ingredient tip: *you can add two leaves of sage to add flavor to the meal.*

Prep	**Portion**	**Cook**	**Per Serving**
10 m	6	2 h	Calories: 273; Protein: 38g; Carbs: 20g; Fat: 3g

HERB CRUSTED TURKEY BREASTS AND VEGGIES

. . . .

2 tsp garlic, minced
1 tbsp parsley, finely chopped
1 tbsp thyme, finely chopped
1 tbsp rosemary, finely chopped
2 lb. turkey breasts, deboned and skinless
3 tsp avocado oil, divided
Salt, ground
Black pepper, ground
2 orange sweet potatoes, big cubes
2 medium carrots, big cubes
2 heads broccoli, cut into florets
1 onion, thinly sliced

Directions:

1. *Heat the oven to 350°F gas mark 4. Cover a large deep roasting pan with aluminum foil. Set it aside.*
2. *In a small mixing bowl, combine the minced garlic, finely chopped parsley, thyme, and rosemary and mix.*
3. *Add the deboned turkey breast into the prepared roasting pan and drizzle with 1 tsp avocado oil and rub the herb mixture all over. Season with ground Salt and ground black pepper.*
4. *Roast the turkey breasts for 30 minutes.*
5. *Then prepare the sweet potato chunks, carrots chunks, broccoli florets, thinly sliced onion, and mix them together with 2 tsp of avocado oil in a large bowl.*
6. *Remove the turkey breasts from the oven and place the vegetables around them.*
7. *Place the turkey breasts with the vegetables back in the oven and roast for 1½ hours until the turkey breasts are cooked and the vegetables are tender.*

Substitution tip: *You can use chicken breasts in place of the turkey breasts.*

SEAFOOD

SCAN ME! RECIPES' COLOR IMAGES

Prep
3 m

Portion
4

Cook
8 m

Per Serving
330 Calories, 15g fat, 2g Carbs,
45g Protein

PAN-SEARED SESAME-CRUSTED TUNA STEAKS

¾ cup sesame seeds
4 (6-ounce) skinless tuna steaks, 1 inch thick
2 tbsp canola oil
¼ tsp salt
⅛ tsp pepper

Directions:
1.   Spread sesame seeds in shallow baking dish. Pat tuna steaks dry with paper towels, rub steaks all over with 1 tbsp oil, then sprinkle with salt and pepper. Press both sides of each steak in sesame seeds to coat.
2.   Heat remaining 1 tbsp oil in 12-inch nonstick skillet over medium-high heat until just smoking. Place steaks in skillet and cook until seeds are golden and tuna is translucent red at center when checked with tip of paring knife and registers 110 degrees (for rare), 1 to 2 minutes per side. Transfer tuna to cutting board and slice ½ inch thick. Serve.

Substitution tip: you can use extra-virgin oil to replace canola oil.

Prep
5 m

Portion
4

Cook
10 m

Per Serving
360 Calories, 24g fat, 0g Carbs,
35g Protein

OVER-ROASTED SALMON

OVEN-ROASTED SALMON

1 (1½-pound) skin-on salmon fillet, 1 inch thick
1 tsp extra-virgin olive oil
¼ tsp salt
⅛ tsp pepper

Directions:
1.	Adjust oven rack to lowest position, place aluminum foil–lined rimmed baking sheet on rack, and heat oven to 500 degrees. Cut salmon crosswise into 4 fillets, then make 4 or 5 shallow slashes about an inch apart along skin side of each piece, being careful not to cut into flesh. Pat fillets dry with paper towels, rub with oil, and sprinkle with salt and pepper.
2.	Once oven reaches 500 degrees, reduce oven temperature to 275 degrees. Remove sheet from oven and carefully place salmon, skin-side down, on hot sheet. Roast until centers are still translucent when checked with tip of paring knife and register 125 degrees (for medium-rare), 4 to 6 minutes.
3.	Slide spatula along underside of fillets and transfer to individual serving plates or serving platter, leaving skin behind; discard skin. Serve.

Prep
5 m

Portion
4

Cook
5 m

Per Serving
Calories 252 Carbs 7g Protein 39g
Fat 7g

BLACKENED SHRIMP

1 ½ lbs. shrimp, peel & devein
4 lime wedges
4 tbsp. cilantro, chopped
What you'll need from store cupboard:
4 cloves garlic, diced
1 tbsp. chili powder
1 tbsp. paprika
1 tbsp. exatra-virgin olive oil
2 tsp Splenda brown sugar
1 tsp cumin
1 tsp oregano
1 tsp garlic powder
1 tsp salt
½ tsp pepper

Directions:
1.   In a small bowl combine seasonings and
Splenda brown sugar.
2.   Heat oil in a skillet over med-high heat. Add
shrimp, in a single layer, and cook 1-2 minutes per
side.
3.   Add seasonings, and cook, stirring, 30 seconds.
Serve garnished with cilantro and a lime wedge.

Substitution tip: replace Splenda brown sugar with
stevia.

Type 2 Diabetes Cookbook

Prep
10 m

Portion
8 Makes (2
CRAB CAKES
PER SERVING)

Cook
10 m

Per Serving
Calories 96 Carbs 3g Protein 12g
Fat 4g

CRAB CAKES

. . . .

lb. lump blue crabmeat
tbsp. red bell pepper, diced fine
tbsp. green bell pepper, diced fine
tbsp. fresh parsley, chopped fine
eggs
4 tsp fresh lemon juice
What you'll need from store cupboard:
4 cup + 1 tbsp. lite mayonnaise
4 cup Dijon mustard
tbsp. sunflower oil
tbsp. baking powder
tbsp. Worcestershire sauce
½ tsp Old Bay

Directions:

In a small bowl, whisk together ¼ cup
mayonnaise, Dijon mustard, Worcestershire, and
lemon juice until combined. Cover and chill until
ready to serve.

2.   In a large bowl, mix crab, bell peppers, parsley,
eggs, 1 tbsp mayonnaise, baking powder, and Old
Bay seasoning until Ingredients are combined.
3.   Heat oil in a large skillet over med-high heat.
Once oil is hot, drop 2 tbsp crab mixture into hot
skillet. They will be loose but as the egg cooks, they
will hold together.
4.   Cook 2 minutes or until firm, then flip and cook
another minute. Transfer to serving plate. Serve with
mustard dipping sauce.

Substitution tip: *replace Dijon mustard with light
mayonnaise.*

Prep
5 m

Portion
4

Cook
20 m

Per Serving
Calories 408 Carbs 4g Protein 41g
Fat 24g

BAKED SALMON WITH GARLIC PARMESAN TOPPING

. . . .

1 lb. wild caught salmon filets
2 tbsp low fat margarine
What you'll need from store cupboard:
¼ cup reduced fat parmesan cheese, grated
¼ cup light mayonnaise
2-3 cloves garlic, diced
2 tbsp parsley
Salt and pepper

Directions:
1.   *Heat oven to 350 and line a baking pan with parchment paper.*
2.   *Place salmon on pan and season with salt and pepper.*
3.   *In a medium skillet, over medium heat, melt butter. Add garlic and cook, stirring 1 minute.*
4.   *Reduce heat to low and add remaining Ingredients. Stir until everything is melted and combined.*
5.   *Spread evenly over salmon and bake 15 minutes for thawed fish or 20 for frozen. Salmon is done when it flakes easily with a fork. Serve.*

Substitution: *you can replace salmon with cod fish.*

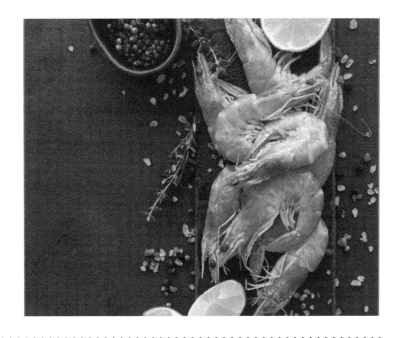

Prep
5 m

Portion
4

Cook
10 m

Per Serving
Calories 283 Carbs 15g Protein
28g Fat 12g

CRUNCHY LEMON SHRIMP

1 lb. raw shrimp, peeled and deveined
2 tbsp. Italian parsley, roughly chopped
2 tbsp. lemon juice, divided
What you'll need from store cupboard:
⅔ cup panko bread crumbs
2½ tbsp extra-virgin olive oil, divided
Salt and pepper, to taste

Directions:
1.   Heat oven to 400 degrees.
2.   Place the shrimp evenly in a baking dish and sprinkle with salt and pepper. Drizzle on 1 tbsp lemon juice and 1 tbsp of olive oil. Set aside.
3.   In a medium bowl, combine parsley, remaining lemon juice, bread crumbs, remaining olive oil, and ¼ tsp each of salt and pepper. Layer the panko mixture evenly on top of the shrimp.
4.   Bake 8-10 minutes or until shrimp are cooked through and the panko is golden brown.

Prep
2 h

Portion
4

Cook
0 m

Per Serving
Calories: 375; Protein: 50g; Carbs:
8g; Fat: 16g

USA SUSHI TUNA

. . . .

2 lb. fresh tuna, sushi-grade cut into cubes
1 cup spring onion, thinly sliced
1 cup dark soy sauce
¼ cup sesame oil
1 tbsp ginger, grated
Salt, ground
Black pepper, ground
1 tbsp sesame seeds, lightly toasted

Directions:
1.   *In a medium bowl, add the cubed tuna, sliced spring onion, dark soy sauce, sesame oil, and grated ginger. Season with ground Salt and ground black pepper.*
2.   *Sprinkle over toasted sesame seeds and cover. Place in the fridge for 2 hours or more before serving.*

Ingredient tip: *add sesame seeds to add flavor to your dish.*

Prep
4 h

Portion
4

Cook
0 m

Per Serving
Calories: 108; Fat: 1g; Protein: 21g;
Carbs: 4g;

LIME AND SEA BASS

. . . .

1 lb. sushi-grade sea bass, chopped and chilled
1½ cups cherry tomatoes, quartered
1 cup lime juice
¾ cup coriander, finely chopped
¼ cup onion, finely chopped
Sea salt, ground
Black pepper, ground

Directions:
1. In a glass mixing bowl, add the chopped sea bass, quartered cherry tomatoes, lime juice, chopped coriander, and finely chopped onion. Season with ground sea salt and ground black pepper and mix.
2. Marinate the mixture in a fridge for 4 hours or overnight.
3. Serve chilled and enjoy!

Substitution tip: sea bass can be replaced with snapper.

Prep	**Portion**	**Cook**	**Per Serving**
5 m	4	12-13 m	180 Calories, 9g fat, 3g Carbs, 22g Protein

SALMON WITH LEMON-THYME SLICES

. . . .

2 medium lemons
4 (4-ounce) salmon fillets, rinsed and patted dry, skinned (if desired)
1/2 tsp dried thyme, crushed
1/4 tsp salt
1/4 tsp black pepper

Directions:
1.   Preheat the oven to 400°F.
2.   Line a baking sheet with foil and coat with nonstick cooking spray. Slice one of the lemons into 8 rounds and arrange on the baking sheet.
3.   Place the salmon on top of the lemon slices, spray the salmon lightly with nonstick cooking spray, and sprinkle evenly with the thyme, salt, and pepper. Bake the salmon 10–12 minutes or until it flakes with a fork.
4.   Cut the other lemon in quarters and squeeze lemon juice evenly over all.

Substitution tip: *replace salmon with cod fish or tuna.*

Prep
5 m

Portion
4

Cook
10 m

Per Serving
Calories: 382; Fat: 18g; Protein:
48g; Carbs: 7g

SHRIMP AND HALIBUT SAUTÉ

. . . .

1 lb. large shrimps, de-shelled and de-veined
1 lb. halibut fillet, at room temperature
Salt, ground
Black pepper, ground
1 tbsp extra virgin olive oil
4 tbsp plant-based butter
¼ cup garlic, chopped
16 oz baby spinach
1 lemon, quartered

Directions:
1.   Season the shrimp and halibut with ground Salt and ground black pepper.
2.   In a heavy bottom pan over medium heat, warm the olive oil. Fry the halibut fillet for 5 minutes, until lightly browned. Add the shrimp and cook for 3 to 5 minutes turning the shrimp and the fillet occasionally, until completely cooked. Remove from the pan and set aside.
3.   In the same pan add the plant-based butter and chopped garlic and cook, stirring, for 1 minute. Add the baby spinach and season with ground Salt and ground black pepper and mix until the baby spinach has wilted. Turn off the heat.
4.   Distribute the baby spinach evenly between 4 plates and top it with the shrimp and halibut fillet.
5.   Serve warm with a lemon quarter on the side for garnish.

Ingredient tip: Seasoning a fish fillet with salt helps to draw out moisture and helps to firm up the fish when you are frying it.

Prep
5 m

Portion
4

Cook
20 m

Per Serving
Calories: 262; Fat: 11g; Carbs: 4g;
Protein: 32g

PISTACHIOS AND HERB HALIBUT

. . . .

4 (5-oz) halibut fillets, lightly salted
2 tbsp olive oil, for coating
½ cup pistachios, unsalted and finely ground
1 tbsp parsley, finely chopped
1 tsp thyme, chopped
1 tsp basil, finely chopped
Pinch of Salt, ground
Black pepper, ground

Directions:
1 Warm the oven to 350°F gas mark 4. Cover the baking sheet with aluminum foil, set it aside.
2 Dry the halibut fillets with paper towels and place them on the baking sheet.
3 Coat the dried halibut fillets with olive oil.
4 In a small mixing bowl, add the finely ground pistachios, chopped parsley, chopped thyme, finely chopped basil, ground Salt, and ground black pepper, mix to combine.
5 Spoon the pistachio and herb mixture onto the halibut fish, spreading it out so the tops of the halibut fillets are covered.
6 Bake for 20 minutes until the halibut flakes when pressed with a fork
7 Serve warm.

Substitution tip: Cod would be a great fish to use in this recipe.

Prep
15 m

Portion
4

Cook
25 m

Per Serving
Calories 338 Carbs 10g Protein
38g Fat 14g

FISHERMAN'S PIE

. . . .

12 shrimp, peel & de-vein
8 oz. cod, cut in 1-inch pieces
4 oz. salmon, cut in 1-inch pieces
1 slice bacon
4 cup cheesy cauliflower puree
½ cup onion, diced
¼ cup heavy cream
2 tbsp. butter
1 tbsp. fresh parsley, diced
What you'll need from store cupboard:
1 cup low sodium vegetable broth
½ cup dry white wine
1 clove garlic, diced fine
¼ tsp celery salt
Salt & pepper, to taste
Non-stick cooking spray

Directions:

1.   Heat oven to 400 degrees. Spray a large casserole dish, or 4 small ones with cooking spray.
2.   Melt butter in a medium saucepan over medium heat. Add onion and cook until soft. Add the garlic and cook 1 minute more.
3.   Pour in the wine and broth and cook 5 minutes.
4.   Stir in cream, bacon, and celery salt and simmer 5 minutes, until bacon is cooked through and most of the fat has rendered off. Remove the slice of bacon, chop it up and add it back to the pot.
5.   Add the seafood, parsley, salt, and pepper to taste and simmer 2-3 minutes. Transfer mixture to prepared casserole dish.
6.   Place the cauliflower in a large Ziploc bag, or pastry bag, and snip off one corner. Pipe the cauliflower in small rosettes to cover the top. Bake 8-10 minutes, or until heated through and top is lightly browned, you may need to broil it for 1-2 minutes to reach the browned color. Serve.
e.

Prep
5 m

Portion
2

Cook
35 m

Per Serving
(1 fillet with 2 cups vegetables):
Calories: 286; Fat: 13g; Carbs: 12g;
Protein: 26g

ROASTED COD AND FRENCH STEW

· ·

½ eggplant, chopped
2 zucchini, chopped
3 tomatoes, chopped
1 red or green bell pepper chopped
½ red onion, sliced
3 tsp garlic, crushed
2 tbsp avocado oil
2 tsp oregano, dried
¼ tsp cayenne pepper, fresh or ground
2 (6oz) cod fillets, lightly salted
Salt, ground
Black pepper, ground
½ cup feta, crumbled

Directions:
1.   Warm oven to 400°F gas mark 6. Place aluminum foil on a baking sheet.
2.   In a large mixing bowl, add the chopped eggplant, chopped zucchini, chopped tomatoes, chopped red or green bell pepper, sliced red onion, crushed garlic, avocado oil, dried oregano, and fresh or ground cayenne pepper and mix until well combined.
3.   Spread the vegetable mixture in the center of the baking sheet and bake for 25 minutes tuning the vegetables halfway.
4.   Season the cod fillets with ground Salt and ground black pepper and place the fish fillets on top of the vegetables, baking them for a further 10 minutes.
5.   Serve the cod and vegetables hot and topped with crumbled feta.

Substitution tip: You can use crumbled ricotta cheese in place of feta cheese.

Prep	**Portion**	**Cook**	**Per Serving**
10 m	4	25 m	Calories 448 Carbs 12g Protein 29g fat 30g

SHRIMP IN COCONUT CURRY

. . . .

1 lb. extra-large shrimp, peel & de-vein
1 onion, diced fine
1 ¾ cup coconut milk, unsweetened
2 tbsp. fresh lemon juice
1 tbsp. fresh ginger, grated
What you'll need from store cupboard:
14.5 oz. can tomatoes, diced
3 cloves garlic, diced fine
1 tbsp. coconut oil
2 tsp coriander
1 tsp curry powder
1 tsp salt, or to taste
½ tsp turmeric
¾ tsp black pepper
¼ tsp cayenne

Directions:

1.   In a medium bowl combine lemon juice, ¼ tsp salt, ¼ tsp pepper and the cayenne pepper. Add shrimp and toss to coat. Cover and refrigerate at least 10 minutes.
2.   Heat the oil in a large, deep, skillet over med-high heat. Add onion and cook until it starts to soften, about 2-3 minutes. Add remaining seasonings and cook 1 minute more.
3.   Add tomatoes with juices and coconut milk, stir and bring to boil. Cook, stirring occasionally, 5 minutes.
4.   Add shrimp and marinade and cook till shrimp turn pink about 2-3 minutes. Serve.

BEEF, PORK AND LAMB

SCAN ME! RECIPES' COLOR IMAGES

Prep	**Portion**	**Cook**	**Per Serving**
5 m	6	30 m	Calorie: 265 fat: 13g Protein: 31g Carbs: 3g

PORK CHOPS POMODORO

. . . .

2 pounds (907 g) boneless pork loin chops, each about 5⅓ ounces and ½ inch thick
¾ tsp fine sea salt
½ tsp freshly ground black pepper
2 tbsp extra-virgin olive oil
2 garlic cloves, chopped
½ cup low-sodium chicken broth or vegetable broth
½ tsp Italian seasoning
1 tbsp capers, drained
2 cups cherry tomatoes
2 tbsp chopped fresh basil or flat-leaf parsley
Spiralized zucchini noodles, cooked cauliflower "rice," or cooked whole-grain pasta for serving
Lemon wedges for serving

Directions

1. Pat the pork chops dry with paper towels, then season them all over with the salt and pepper. 2. Select the Sauté setting on the Instant Pot and heat 1 tbsp of the oil for 2 minutes. Swirl the oil to coat the bottom of the pot. Using tongs, add half of the pork chops in a single layer and sear for about 3 minutes, until lightly browned on the first side. Flip the chops and sear for about 3 minutes more, until lightly browned on the second side. Transfer the chops to a plate. Repeat with the remaining 1 tbsp oil and pork chops. 3. Add the garlic to the pot and sauté for about 1 minute, until bubbling but not browned. Stir in the broth, Italian seasoning, and capers, using a wooden spoon to nudge any browned bits from the bottom of the pot and working quickly so not too much liquid evaporates. Using the tongs, transfer the pork chops to the pot. Add the tomatoes in an even layer on top of the chops. 4. Secure the lid and set the Pressure Release to Sealing. Press the Cancel button to reset the cooking program, then select the Pressure Cook or Manual setting and set the cooking time for 10 minutes at high pressure. (The pot will take about 5 minutes to come up to pressure before the cooking program begins.) 5. When the cooking program ends, let the pressure release naturally for at least 10 minutes, then move the Pressure Release to Venting to release any remaining steam. Open the pot and, using the tongs, transfer the pork chops to a serving dish. 6. Spoon the tomatoes and some of the cooking liquid on top of the pork chops. Sprinkle with the basil and serve right away, with zucchini noodles and lemon wedges on the side.

Substitution tip: you can use beef to replace pork.

Prep
5 m

Portion
4

Cook
5 m

Per Serving
170 Calories, 7g fat, 0g Carbs, 25g
Protein

PAN-SEARED SIRLOIN STEAK

1 (1-pound) boneless beef top sirloin steak, 1 to 1½ inches thick, trimmed of all visible fat
¼ tsp salt
⅛ tsp pepper
2 tsp canola oil
Lemon wedges

Directions:
1.   Pat steak dry with paper towels and sprinkle with salt and pepper. Heat oil in 12-inch skillet over medium-high heat until just smoking. Brown steak well on first side, 3 to 5 minutes.
2.   Flip steak and continue to cook until meat registers 120 to 125 degrees (for medium-rare), 5 to 10 minutes, reducing heat as needed to prevent scorching. Transfer steak to carving board, tent with aluminum foil, and let rest for 5 minutes. Slice steak thin and serve with lemon wedges.

Prep
10 m

Portion
16 Makes

Cook
6 h

Per Serving
Calories 265 Carbs 14g Protein
17g Fat 14g

BBQ PORK TACOS

2 lb. pork shoulder, trim off excess fat
2 onions, diced fine
2 cups cabbages, shredded
What you'll need from store cupboard:
16 (6-inch) low Carbs whole wheat tortillas
4 chipotle peppers in adobo sauce, pureed
1 cup light barbecue sauce
2 cloves garlic, diced fine
1 ½ tsp paprika

Directions:
1.   In a medium bowl, whisk together garlic,
barbecue sauce and chipotles, cover and chill.
2.   Place pork in the crock pot. Cover and cook on
low 8-10 hours, or on high 4-6 hours.
3.   Transfer pork to a cutting board. Use two forks
and shred the pork, discarding the fat. Place pork
back in the crock pot. Sprinkle with paprika then
pour the barbecue sauce over mixture.

4.   Stir to combine, cover and cook 1 hour. Skim off
excess fat.
5.   To assemble the tacos: place about ¼ cup of
pork on warmed tortilla. Top with cabbage and
onions and serve. Refrigerate any leftover pork up to
3 days.
Ingredient tip: if you don't want pork use beef.

Prep
5 m

Portion
4

Cook
15 m

Per Serving
Calories: 332; Protein: 24g; Carbs: 13g; Fat: 19g

BASIL MEATBALL BAKE

Non-stick cooking spray
½ lb. ground pork, lean
½ lb. ground beef, lean
1 onion, finely chopped
¼ cup breadcrumbs
2 tbsp basil, chopped
2 tsp garlic, minced
1 egg
Pinch Salt, ground
Pinch black pepper, ground
Marinara sauce
Vegetable of your choice

Directions:

1.   Heat the oven to 350°F gas mark 4.
2.   Coat a baking tray with non-stick cooking spray and set it aside.
3.   In a large mixing bowl, add the ground pork, ground beef, chopped onion, breadcrumbs, chopped basil, minced garlic, egg, ground Salt, and ground black pepper and mix well to combine.
4.   Roll the ground meat into medium-sized meatballs.
5.   Put the meatballs onto the baking tray and bake for 15 minutes until browned and cooked through.
6.   Serve the meatballs with marinara sauce and some steamed green beans or any vegetable of your choice.

Ingredient tip: You can serve this with spaghetti squash or zucchini noodles.

Prep	**Portion**	**Cook**	**Per Serving**
5 m	4	5 h	Calories: 920; Fat: 72g; Protein: 59g; Carbs: 9g

SLOW-COOKED ORANGE AND PORK SLAW

. . . .

1½ tbsp chili powder, divided
2 tbsp ground cumin, divided
1½ tsp salt, divided
2½ tsp black pepper, divided
2 tbsp orange zest, divided
3–4 lbs. pork shoulder, fat trimmed
6 tsp chopped garlic, divided
Juice of 2 oranges, divided
4 cups green or red cabbage, julienned
½ tbsp extra-virgin olive oil

Directions:

1.   In a small bowl, combine 1 tbsp chili powder, 1 tbsp cumin, 1 tsp salt, 2 tsp black pepper, and 1 tbsp orange zest. Rub the seasoning on the pork shoulder. Set aside.
2.   In a slow cooker, add 5 tsp chopped garlic and the juice of 1 orange and mix. Place the seasoned pork shoulder inside, cover, and cook on low for 8 hours or on high for 5 hours. The pork will break apart when cooked properly.
3.   Remove the cooked pork shoulder and place it in a dish that will gather the running juices. Shred the meat and place it back into the slow cooker along with the juices. Season to taste.
4.   Preheat the oven to broil.
5.   On a baking sheet, place the shredded pork and broil for 3 to 4 minutes, until crispy.
6.   In a large-sized bowl, add the remaining orange juice, chili powder, cumin, garlic, salt, black pepper, and orange zest. Add the julienned cabbage and olive oil, mix well until well combined.

Substitution tip: Swap the Protein for any of your choice.

Tip: If you do not want a citrus flavor, you can add sliced apples in step 2.

Prep
5 m

Portion
4

Cook
22 m

Per Serving
190 Calories, 3g fat, 14g Carbs,
23g Protein

SWEET SHERRY'D PORK TENDERLOIN

· ·

1 pound pork tenderloin
1/4 cup dry sherry (divided use)
3 tbsp lite soy sauce (divided use)
1/3 cup peach all-fruit spread

Directions:
1.   Place the pork, 2 tbsp sherry, and 2 tbsp soy sauce in a quart-sized zippered plastic bag. Seal tightly and toss back and forth to coat evenly. Refrigerate overnight or at least 8 hours.
2.   Stir the fruit spread, 2 tbsp sherry, and 1 tbsp soy sauce together in a small bowl. Cover with plastic wrap and refrigerate until needed.
3.   Preheat the oven to 425°F.
4.   Remove the pork from the marinade and discard the marinade. Place a medium nonstick skillet over medium-high heat until hot. Coat the skillet with nonstick cooking spray, add the pork, and brown on all sides.
5.   Place the pork in a 9-inch pie pan and bake 15 minutes or until the pork is barely pink in the center. Place the pork on a cutting board and let stand 3 minutes before slicing.
6.   Meanwhile, place the fruit spread mixture in the skillet and bring to a boil over medium-high heat, stirring frequently. Place the sauce on the bottom of a serving plate and arrange the pork on top. Sprinkle evenly with black pepper, if desired.

Prep
10 m

Portion
10

Cook
8 h

Per Serving
Calories 445 Carbs 4g Protein
69g Fat 14g

BEER BRAISED BRISKET

. . . .

5 lb. beef brisket
1 bottle of lite beer
1 onion, sliced thin
What you'll need from store cupboard:
15 oz. can tomatoes, diced
3 cloves garlic, diced fine
1 tbsp. + 1 tsp oregano
1 tbsp. salt
1 tbsp. black pepper

Directions:
1.   *Place the onion on the bottom of the crock pot. Add brisket, fat side up. Add the tomatoes, undrained and beer. Sprinkle the garlic and seasonings on the top.*
2.   *Cover and cook on low heat 8 hours, or until beef is fork tender.*

Ingredient tips: *you can add a sliced carrot to add more flavor to your meal.*

Prep	**Portion**	**Cook**	**Per Serving**
5 m	6 Makes	10 m	Calories: 187 fat: 9g Protein: 14g
			Carbs: 14g

QUICK & EASY STEAK TACOS

. . . .

1 tbsp olive oil
8 ounces sirloin steak
2 tbsp steak seasoning
1 tsp Worcestershire sauce
½ red onion, halved and sliced
6 corn tortillas
¼ cup tomatoes
¾ cup reduced-fat Mexican cheese
2 tbsp low-fat sour cream
6 tbsp garden fresh salsa
¼ cup chopped fresh cilantro

Directions:

1. Turn the Instant Pot on the Sauté function. When the pot displays "hot," add the olive oil to the pot.
2. Season the steak with the steak seasoning.
3. Add the steak to the pot along with the Worcestershire sauce.
4. Cook each side of the steak for 2–3 minutes until the steak turns brown.
5. Remove the steak from the pot and slice thinly.
6. Add the onion to the pot with the remaining olive oil and steak juices and cook them until translucent.
7. Remove the onion from the pot.
8. Warm your corn tortillas, then assemble your steak, onion, tomatoes, cheese, sour cream, salsa, and cilantro on top of each.

Substitution tip: *replace Mexican cheese with cheddar.*

Prep
15 m

Portion
6

Cook
10 m

Per Serving
Calorie: 140 fat: 7g Protein: 18g
Carbs: 3g

QUICK & EASY BEEF

. . . .

1 tbsp extra-virgin olive oil
1 small onion, thinly sliced
2 tsp minced fresh ginger
3 garlic cloves, minced
2 tsp ground coriander
1 tsp ground cumin
1 jalapeño or Serrano pepper, slit lengthwise but not all the way through
¼ tsp ground turmeric
¼ tsp salt
1 pound (454 g) grass-fed sirloin tip steak, top round steak, or top sirloin steak, cut into bite-size pieces
2 tbsp chopped fresh cilantro

Directions

1. In a large skillet, heat the oil over medium high.
2. Add the onion, and cook for 3 to 5 minutes until browned and softened. Add the ginger and garlic, stirring continuously until fragrant, about 30 seconds.
3. In a small bowl, mix the coriander, cumin, jalapeño, turmeric, and salt. Add the spice mixture to the skillet and stir continuously for 1 minute. De-glaze the skillet with about ¼ cup of water.
4. Add the beef and stir continuously for about 5 minutes until well-browned yet still medium rare. Remove the jalapeño. Serve topped with the cilantro.

Substitution tip: you can replace beef with chicken.

Prep
5 m

Portion
8

Cook
1 h 15 m

Per Serving
Calories 327 Carbs 10g Protein
22g Fat 22g

HERB CRUSTED BAKED HAM

· ·

5 lb. smoked ham, bone-in
2 tbsp. fresh rosemary, diced
What you'll need from store cupboard:
1 cup yellow mustard
½ cup lite mayonnaise
2 tbsp. garlic, diced fine
Pepper, to taste

Directions:

1. *Heat oven to 300 degrees.*
2. *Place ham in a roasting pan, fat side up.*
3. *In a small bowl, combine all Ingredients and spread over ham.*
4. *Pour ½ cup water in the bottom of the roaster and bake 1 hour 15 minutes. Let rest 10 minutes before slicing and serving.*

Prep
10 m

Portion
4

Cook
25 m

Per Serving
Calories: 332 fat: 16g Protein: 44g
Carbs: 1g

PARMESAN-CRUSTED PORK CHOPS

. . . .

Non-stick cooking spray
4 bone-in, thin-cut pork chops
2 tbsp butter
½ cup grated Parmesan cheese
3 garlic cloves, minced
¼ tsp salt
¼ tsp dried thyme
Freshly ground black pepper, to taste

Directions

1.   Preheat the oven to 400°F (205°C). Line a baking sheet with parchment paper and spray with nonstick cooking spray.
2. Arrange the pork chops on the prepared baking sheet so they do not overlap.
3. In a small bowl, combine the butter, cheese, garlic, salt, thyme, and pepper. Press 2 tbsp of the cheese mixture onto the top of each pork chop.
4. Bake for 18 to 22 minutes until the pork is cooked through and its juices run clear. Set the broiler to high, then broil for 1 to 2 minutes to brown the tops.

Prep
5 m

Portion
4

Cook
20 m

Per Serving
150 Calories, 3g fat, 8g Carbs, 22g
Protein

SWEET JERK PORK

. . . .

1 pound pork tenderloin
2 tsp jerk seasoning
2 tbsp packed dark brown sugar
2 tsp Worcestershire sauce

Directions:
1.   Preheat the oven to 425°F.
2.   Sprinkle the pork evenly with the jerk seasoning and press down gently so the spices adhere. Let the pork stand 15 minutes.
3.   Stir the sugar and Worcestershire sauce together in a small bowl until well blended. Coat an 11 × 7-inch baking pan with nonstick cooking spray and set aside.
4.   Place a large nonstick skillet over medium-high heat until hot. Coat the skillet with nonstick cooking spray, add the pork, and brown all sides, about 5 minutes, turning occasionally.
5.   Place the pork in the baking pan and spoon all but 1 tbsp of the Worcestershire mixture evenly over the pork. Bake for 13–15 minutes or until the pork is barely pink in the center and a meat thermometer reaches 170°F.
6.   Place the pork on a cutting board, spoon the remaining 1 tbsp Worcestershire mixture evenly over all, and let stand 10 minutes before slicing.

Prep	**Portion**	**Cook**	**Per Serving**
10 m	4	1 h 40 m	Calories: 330; Fat: 18g; Carbs: 4g; Protein: 36g

SHERRY ROASTED BEEF AND PEPPER SAUCE

. . . .

1½ lb. rump beef roast
Salt, fine
Black pepper, ground
3 tsp extra virgin olive oil, divided
3 small onions, minced
2 tsp garlic, minced
1 tbsp green peppercorns
2 tbsp sherry
2 tbsp almond flour
1 cup beef broth, no salt

Directions:

1. Heat the oven to 300°F gas mark 2.
2. Generously season the beef roast with fine Salt and ground black pepper.
3. In a cast-iron pan over medium-high heat add 2 tsp of olive oil and cook until hot.
4. Brown the beef on all sides, about 10 minutes in total, and place it into a baking dish.
5. Roast the beef until cooked to your satisfaction, about 1½ hours for medium cooked. When the roast has been in the oven for 1 hour, start the pepper sauce.
6. In the same pan over medium-high heat, fry the minced onion in the remaining 1 tsp of olive oil for 4 minutes until soft.
7. Stir in the minced garlic and green peppercorns and cook for 1 minute. Whisk in the sherry to deglaze the pan.
8. Whisk in the almond flour to form a thick paste, cook for 1 minute stirring constantly.
9. Add the no-salt beef broth and whisk for 4 minutes until the sauce is thick and glossy. Season the sauce with fine Salt and ground black pepper.
10. Carve and serve the beef with a generous spoonful of sauce.

Ingredient tip: replace almond flour with hazelnut flour.

Prep
5 m

Portion
4

Cook
10 m

Per Serving
Calories: 413; Protein: 31g; Carbs: 1g; Fat: 29g

LIME LAMB CHOPS

. . . .

¼ cup extra virgin olive oil
¼ cup lime juice
2 tbsp lime zest
2 tbsp mint, chopped
2 tbsp parsley, chopped
Pinch of Salt, ground
Pinch black pepper, ground
12 lamb chops

Directions:

1.   In a small mixing bowl, whisk together the olive oil, lime juice, lime zest, chopped parsley, chopped mint, ground Salt, and ground black pepper.
2.   Transfer the mixture into a marinading dish with a lid.
3.   Add the lamb chops into the marinading dish and cover with the lid. Mix to combine.
4.   Place the dish with the marinated lamb for 4 hours in the fridge, turning several times.
5.   Preheat the oven to broil.
6.   Remove the chops from the dish and arrange them on an aluminum foil-lined baking sheet. Discard the remaining marinade.
7.   Broil the lamb chops for 4 minutes on each side.
8.   Rest the lamb chops for 5 minutes before serving.

Ingredient tip: *Mint goes perfectly with lamb. You can cook down the remaining marinade and thicken it into a sauce for the lamb chops.*

SOUPS, STEWS & CHILES

SCAN ME! RECIPES' COLOR IMAGES

Prep
5 m

Portion
4

Cook
40 m

Per Serving
150 Calories, 2g fat,10g Carbs, 24g Protein

TILAPIA STEW WITH GREEN PEPPERS

1 medium green bell pepper, chopped
1 (14.5-ounce) can stewed tomatoes with Italian seasonings
1 cup water
1 pound tilapia filets, rinsed and cut into 1-inch pieces
1/2 tsp seafood seasoning

Directions:

1.   Place a large saucepan over medium heat until hot. Coat the pan with non-stick cooking spray, add the bell pepper, and cook 5 minutes or until beginning to lightly brown, stirring frequently.

2.   Add the tomatoes and water, increase to high heat, and bring to a boil. Reduce the heat, cover tightly, and simmer until the tomatoes are tender. Using the back of a spoon, break up the larger pieces of tomato.

3.   Add the fish and seasonings and stir very gently. Increase the heat to high and bring just to a boil. Reduce the heat, cover tightly, and simmer 3 minutes or until the fish is opaque in the center. Remove from the heat and let stand, covered, 10 minutes to develop flavors.

Prep
5 m

Portion
4

Cook
30 m

Per Serving
Calories: 222; Protein: 14g; Carbs:
19g; Fat: 10g

KALE AND CAULIFLOWER SOUP

2 tbsp avocado oil
8 oz green beans, cut into pieces
10 oz cauliflower, florets
1 tbsp garlic, minced
8 cups vegetable stock
1 can tomatoes, diced
2 cups kale, chopped
Sea salt, ground
Black pepper, ground
1 tbsp parsley, chopped (optional
1 tbsp coriander, chopped (optional)
1 tbsp chives, chopped (optional)
½ lemon, juice (optional)

Directions:
1.	Heat the avocado oil in a large pot over medium heat. Add the cut green beans pieces and cauliflower florets and cook for 7 to 9 minutes, stirring occasionally, until lightly brown. Add the minced garlic and cook for 2 minutes, stirring occasionally.
2.	Increase the heat to high, and add the vegetable stock, diced tomatoes, and chopped kale, and bring to a boil. Reduce the heat to low, let simmer gently for 15 to 20 minutes, until the vegetables are tender.
3.	Season with ground sea salt and ground black pepper. Serve with a sprinkle of fresh parsley, coriander, chives and lemon juice (if using) for extra flavor.

Ingredient tip: if you like it, you can add cumin.

Prep
5 m

Portion
4

Cook
30 m

Per Serving
Calories 537 Carbs 8g Protein 46g
Fat 33g

SALMON DILL SOUP

4 skinless salmon fillets, cut into pieces
1 green onion, diced fine
1 daikon radish, peeled and diced
½ cup heavy cream
2 tbsp. fresh dill, diced
2 tbsp. margarine
What you'll need from store cupboard:
4 cups seafood stock or vegetable broth
½ cup white wine
Salt and black pepper

Directions:
1.   In a large saucepan, melt margarine over med-high heat. Add onions and sauté for 1-2 minutes.
2.   Add wine and cook until liquid is reduced by half.
3.   Add the radish and broth. Cook until radish is tender, about 15 minutes. Add salmon, cream and dill and cook another 5-8 minutes until salmon is flaky. Salt and pepper to taste.

Substitution tip: codfish is delicious too with this recipe.

Prep
5 m

Portion
6

Cook
7 h

Per Serving
Calories 213 Carbs 9g Protein 29g
Fat 6g

BEEF AND LENTIL SOUP

. . . .

1 ½ lbs. beef stew meat
1 cup onion, diced
½ cup celery, diced
What you'll need from store cupboard:
6 cup water
½ cup lentils
2 cloves garlic, diced
2 bay leaves
2 tsp salt
1 tsp extra virgin olive oil
Fresh ground black pepper

Directions:
1.	*In a large skillet over med-high heat, heat oil. Add beef and brown on all sides. Use a slotted spoon to transfer the meat to a crock pot.*
2.	*Add remaining Ingredients, cover and cook on low 6-7 hours or until beef is tender. Discard bay leaves before serving.*
Ingredient tip: *a nice touch is to add Laurel leaves.*

Prep	**Portion**	**Cook**	**Per Serving**
10 m	6	35 m	Calories 210 Carbs 15g Protein 23g Fat 7g

CHUNKY CHICKEN NOODLE SOUP

. . . .

2 lbs. chicken thighs, boneless and skinless
2 carrots, sliced
2 celery stalks, sliced
2 tsp fresh ginger, grated
What you'll need from store cupboard:
8 cup low sodium chicken broth
2 cup homemade pasta, (chapter 15)
1 tbsp. garlic, diced fine
1 tbsp. chicken bouillon
Salt and pepper, to taste

Directions:

1.   Place chicken and 1 cup broth in a large soup pot over medium heat. Bring to a simmer and cook until chicken is done, about 20 minutes. Transfer chicken to a bowl and shred using 2 forks.

2.   Add the carrots, celery, garlic, ginger, and bouillon to the pot and stir well. Add in remaining broth and bring back to a boil. Reduce heat and simmer until vegetables are tender, about 15 minutes.

3.   Add pasta and cook another 5 minutes for fresh pasta, or 7 for dried. Add the chicken to the soup and salt and pepper to taste. Serve.

Substitution tip: *replace noodles with rice.*

Prep	**Portion**	**Cook**	**Per Serving**
5 m	4	25 m	150 Calories, 5g fat, 16g Carbs, 13g Protein

GREEN PEPPER SKILLET CHILI

. . . .

1 pound 93% lean ground beef
1 large green bell pepper, chopped (about 1 1/2 cups total)
1 (14.5-ounce) can stewed no-added-salt tomatoes with liquid
1 (1.25-ounce) packet chili seasoning mix
3/4 cup water

Directions:

1.   Place a large non-stick skillet over medium-high heat until hot. Coat the skillet with non-stick cooking spray, add the beef, and cook until no longer pink, stirring frequently. Set aside on a separate plate.

2.   Recoat the skillet with non-stick cooking spray, add the peppers, and cook 5 minutes or until the edges begin to brown, stirring frequently.

3.   Add the remaining ingredients to the skillet and bring to a boil. Reduce the heat, cover tightly, and simmer 15 minutes or until peppers are very tender, stirring occasionally, using the back of a spoon to crush the tomatoes while cooking.

4.   Remove from the heat and let stand 10 minutes to develop flavors.

Prep	**Portion**	**Cook**	**Per Serving**
5 m	4-6	20 m	Calories: 87; Fat: 3g; Carbs: 13g; Protein: 3g

ZUCCHINI AND TOMATO STEW

. . . .

1 tbsp plant-based butter
2 medium white onions, diced
3 cups (12 oz) zucchini, trimmed and sliced
2½ cups medium tomatoes, cored and chopped
1 tsp Cajun seasoning

Directions:

1.   In a large cast-iron pan, melt the plant-based butter over medium heat.
2.   Add the diced onion and fry until translucent and lightly browned.
3.   Add the sliced zucchini and fry for 5 minutes, until browned.
4.   Mix in the chopped tomatoes and Cajun seasoning and cook for 10 minutes until the zucchini is tender and the tomatoes have broken down.

Prep	**Portion**	**Cook**	**Per Serving**
10 m	6	3 h 35 m	Calories 336 Carbs 8g Protein 37g Fat 17g

SOUTHWEST CHICKEN SOUP

. . . .

2 lbs. boneless skinless chicken breasts
1 onion, diced
1 green pepper, diced
6 oz. reduced fat cream cheese
½ cup half-n-half
1 tbsp. margarine
What you'll need from store cupboard:
2 (10 oz.) cans diced tomatoes with green chilies
3 ½ cup low sodium chicken broth, divided
3 cloves garlic, diced fine
1 packet of taco seasoning
Salt and pepper to taste

Directions:

1.   Place chicken in a crock pot with 1 cup broth. Cover and cook on high 3 hours. Season with salt and pepper.

2.   When chicken is cooked through remove from crock pot and shred.
3.   In a large saucepan, heat butter over medium heat until melted. Add green pepper, onion, and garlic and cook until onion is translucent.
4.   Use a spoon to squash the cream cheese into the veggies so it will melt and Ingredients will come together easily.
5.   Once the cream cheese is melted, add the remaining Ingredients. Simmer on low heat for 20 minutes.
6.   Add chicken, cover and simmer another 10 minutes. Serve garnished with grated cheese, chopped cilantro, or a dollop of sour cream if desired.

Prep
5 m

Portion
6

Cook
1 h

Per Serving
Calories 580 Carbs 5g Protein
34g Fat 46g

SAUSAGE AND PEPPER SOUP

. . . .

2 lbs. pork sausage
10 oz. raw spinach
1 medium bell pepper, diced
What you'll need from store cupboard:
4 cups low sodium beef broth
1 can tomatoes w/ jalapenos
1 tbsp. olive oil
1 tbsp. chili powder
1 tbsp. cumin
1 tsp onion powder
1 tsp garlic powder
1 tsp Italian seasoning
3/4 tsp kosher salt

Directions:
1.   In a large pot, over medium heat, heat oil until hot. Add sausage and cook until browned. Drain fat.
2.   Add bell pepper and stir. Season with salt and pepper.
3.   Add tomatoes and stir. Place spinach on top and cover. Once spinach wilts, add spices and broth and stir to combine.
4.   Reduce heat to medium-low. Cover and cook 30 minutes, stirring occasionally.
5.   Remove lid and let simmer another 15 minutes. Serve.

Prep	**Portion**	**Cook**	**Per Serving**
10 m	4	20 m	Calories: 479; Fat: 18g; Carbs: 17g; Protein: 57g

ITALIAN FISH STEW

. . . .

3 tbsp extra-virgin olive oil
1 brown onion, diced
3 tbsp garlic, minced
½ cup plum tomatoes, roughly chopped
¼ tsp red pepper flakes
2 tbsp tomato paste
½ cup white wine
8 cups vegetable broth or seafood stock
1½ lb. clams or mussels, scrubbed and debearded
1 lb. cod fillets, cut into pieces
½ lb. large shrimp, peeled and deveined
Sea salt, ground
Black pepper, ground
2 scallions, thinly sliced
½ bunch parsley, finely chopped
½ lemon, juiced

Directions:

1. Heat the olive oil in a large stockpot over medium-high heat until hot.
2. Add the diced onion, and cook for 5 minutes, until softened.
3. Add the minced garlic, chopped tomatoes, and red pepper flakes, and cook for 2 minutes, until fragrant.
4. Add the tomato paste, and cook for 2 minutes, until caramelized.
5. Pour in the white wine and vegetable or seafood broth and bring it to a simmer.
6. Add the clean clams or mussels and cook for 5 minutes covered with a lid.
7. Add the cod fillets and replace the lid and cook for 2 minutes.
8. Mix in the peeled shrimp and replace the lid and cook for 3 minutes. The mussels should all be open by then. The mussels that are not open after 10 minutes should be discarded. Season with ground sea salt and ground black pepper.
9. Mix in the chopped scallions, chopped parsley, and lemon juice just before serving.

Substitution tip: you can use any firm, white fish like halibut in this recipe.

Prep
5 m

Portion
4

Cook
13 m

Per Serving
160 Calories, 6g fat, 1g Carbs, 24g Protein

DIJON'D CHICKEN WITH ROSEMARY

· ·

1 tbsp Dijon mustard
1 tbsp extra virgin olive oil
1/4 tsp dried rosemary
4 (4-ounce) boneless, skinless chicken breasts, rinsed and patted dry

Directions:

1.   Using a fork, stir the mustard, olive oil, and rosemary together in a small bowl until well blended and set aside.
2.   Place a medium nonstick skillet over medium heat until hot. Coat the skillet with nonstick cooking spray, add the chicken, and cook 5 minutes.
3.   Turn the chicken, then spoon equal amounts of the mustard mixture over each piece. Reduce the heat to medium low, cover tightly, and cook 7 minutes or until the chicken is no longer pink in the center.
4.   Turn the chicken several times to blend the mustard mixture with the pan drippings, place the chicken on a serving platter, and spoon the mustard mixture over all.

Substitution tips: you can replace Dijon mustard with light mayonnaise.

Prep
5 m

Portion
4

Cook
15 m

Per Serving
Calories: 473; Protein: 46g; Carbs: 12g; Fat: 27g

CREAM OF CHICKEN AND MUSHROOM SOUP

· ·

2 tbsp coconut oil
1½ lb. chicken breast, cubed
1 onion, finely diced
2 cups mushrooms, sliced
½ tbsp garlic, minced
4 cups chicken stock
1 cup milk, low fat
1 cup heavy cream
Sea salt, ground
Black pepper, ground

Directions:

1.   In a pot over medium heat, warm the olive oil and add the cubed chicken, diced onion, sliced mushrooms, and minced garlic cook stirring until the chicken begins to brown.

2.   Add the chicken stock, low-fat milk, and heavy cream, and reduce to a simmer on low for 10 minutes until the chicken is cooked through. Sprinkle with chopped parsley, ground sea salt, and ground black pepper to taste.
Ingredient tip: Adding the chopped parsley adds a completely different taste to the chicken soup.

Ingredient tips: you can add 2 tbsp parsley, finely chopped.

Prep	**Portion**	**Cook**	**Per Serving**
5 m	6	15 m	Calories 336 Carbs 5g Protein 14g Fat 29g

ITALIAN SAUSAGE SOUP

1 lb. pork sausage, cooked
2 cup half-n-half
1 ½ cup cauliflower, grated and cooked
½ cup onion, diced
¼ cup margarine
What you'll need from store cupboard:
1 cup chicken broth
4 cloves garlic, diced fine
1 tsp salt

½ tsp black pepper

Directions:
1.   In a large saucepan, over medium heat, melt margarine. Add onion and garlic, cook, stirring occasionally, 1-2 minutes.
2.   Pour in the broth and cream. Bring to a boil stirring constantly.
3.   Add sausage and cauliflower and season with salt and pepper. Heat through and serve.
Ingredient tip: if you like it, you can add Laurel leaves.

Prep	**Portion**	**Cook**	**Per Serving**
5 m	4	8 h	250 Calories, 12g fat, 12g Carbs, 24g Protein

MEXICAN CHICKEN AND RICE

1 pound boneless, skinless chicken thighs, trimmed of fat
1 (10-ounce) can diced tomatoes with green chilies
3/4 cup instant brown rice
2 tbsp extra-virgin olive oil

Directions:
1.   Combine chicken and tomatoes in a 3 1/2 to 4-quart slow cooker, cover, and cook on low setting for 7–8 hours or on high setting for 3 1/2–4 hours.
2.   Gently stir in rice and 3/4 cup hot water, cover, and cook on high for 20 minutes.
3.   Drizzle oil evenly over all and sprinkle with 1/8 tsp salt.

ONLY VEGETARIAN MEALS

SCAN ME! RECIPES' COLOR IMAGES

Prep	**Portion**	**Cook**	**Per Serving**
5 m	4	13 m	160 Calories, 6g fat, 1g Carbs, 24g Protein

BALSAMIC BEAN SALSA SALAD

. . . .

15-ounce can black beans, rinsed and drained
1/2 cup chopped red bell pepper
1/4 cup finely chopped red onion
2 tbsp balsamic vinegar

Directions:

1. Toss all ingredients in a medium bowl.
2. Let stand 15 minutes to develop flavors.

Prep	**Portion**	**Cook**	**Per Serving**
15 m	4	20 m	Calorie: 261 fat: 17g Protein: 11g Carbs: 18g

MUSHROOM CUTLETS WITH CREAMY SAUCE

. . . .

FOR THE SAUCE
1 tbsp extra-virgin olive oil
2 tbsp whole-wheat flour
1½ cups unsweetened plain almond milk
¼ tsp salt
Dash Worcestershire sauce
Pinch cayenne pepper
¼ cup shredded cheddar cheese
FOR THE CUTLETS
2 eggs
2 cups chopped mushrooms
1 cup quick oats
2 scallions, both white and green parts, chopped
¼ cup shredded cheddar cheese
½ tsp salt
¼ tsp freshly ground black pepper
1 tbsp extra-virgin olive oil

Directions:
TO MAKE THE SAUCE:
1. In a medium saucepan, heat the oil over medium heat. Add the flour and stir constantly for about 2 minutes until browned.
2. Slowly whisk in the almond milk and bring to a boil. Reduce the heat to low and simmer for 6 to 8 minutes until the sauce thickens.
3. Season with the salt, Worcestershire sauce, and cayenne. Add the cheese and stir until melted. Turn off the heat and cover to keep warm while you make the cutlets.
TO MAKE THE CUTLETS
1. In a large mixing bowl, beat the eggs. Add the mushrooms, oats, scallions, cheese, salt, and pepper. Stir to combine.
2. Using your hands, form the mixture into 8 patties, each about ½ inch thick. 3. In a large skillet, heat the oil over medium-high heat. Cook the patties, in batches, if necessary, for 3 minutes per side until crisp and brown.
4. Serve the cutlets warm with sauce drizzled over the top.

Prep
5 m

Portion
4

Cook
20 m

Per Serving
Calories: 244; Fat: 17g; Carbs: 9g;
Protein: 11g

SHERRY TOFU AND SPINACH STIR-FRY

. . . . .

1 (14 oz) block firm tofu, pressed, and cubed
2 tbsp olive oil, divided
Sea salt, fine
1 tbsp sesame oil, toasted
1 onion, thinly sliced
1 bunch spinach, stems removed and thinly sliced
1 tbsp garlic, minced
1 tsp ginger, grated
¼ tsp red pepper flakes
¼ cup low-salt soy sauce
2 tbsp sherry
1 (20 oz) can pineapple chunks, drained
2 scallions, finely sliced
2 tbsp sesame seeds, toasted

Directions:

1.   Heat the oven to 425°F gas mark 7. Cover a deep baking sheet with aluminum foil.
2.   In a large mixing bowl, toss the tofu cubes with 1 tbsp of olive oil, being careful not to break them. Spread onto the baking sheet. Season with fine sea salt.

3.   Place the baking sheet into the oven, and bake the tofu for 13 minutes, until gently browned.
4.   Turn the tofu over and bake for 4 minutes to brown the other side.
5.   In the meantime, add the remaining 1 tbsp olive oil and sesame oil into a heavy bottom pan over high heat until hot.
6.   Add the sliced onion and fry for 4 minutes, until lightly brown.
7.   Bring the heat down to medium and add the sliced spinach and cook for 2 to 3 minutes, until the leaves soften.
8.   Mix in the minced garlic, grated ginger, and red pepper flakes, and cook for 1 minute.
9.   In a small mixing bowl, whisk the low-salt soy sauce, sherry, and pineapple chunks.
10.   Add the sliced scallions and soy sauce mixture to the pan and cook for 5 minutes, stirring frequently until the spinach is cooked and the flavor is incorporated.
11.   Add the tofu to the vegetables and gently mix. Sprinkle with the toasted sesame seeds.

Prep
10 m

Portion
2

Cook
30 m

Per Serving
Calories 134 Total Carbs 22g
Protein 10g Fat 0g

CAULIFLOWER MUSHROOM RISOTTO

1 medium head cauliflower, grated
8 oz. Porcini mushrooms, sliced
1 yellow onion, diced fine
What you'll need from store cupboard:
2 cup low sodium vegetable broth
2 tsp garlic, diced fine
2 tsp white wine vinegar
Salt & pepper, to taste
Olive oil cooking spray

Directions:
1.   Heat oven to 350 degrees. Line a baking sheet with foil.
2.   Place the mushrooms on the prepared pan and spray with cooking spray. Sprinkle with salt and toss to coat. Bake 10-12 minutes, or until golden brown and the mushrooms start to crisp.
3.   Spray a large skillet with cooking spray and place over med-high heat. Add onion and cook, stirring frequently, until translucent, about 3-4 minutes. Add garlic and cook 2 minutes, until golden.

4.   Add the cauliflower and cook 1 minute, stirring.
5.   Place the broth in a saucepan and bring to a simmer. Add to the skillet, ¼ cup at a time, mixing well after each addition.
6.   Stir in vinegar. Reduce heat to low and let simmer, 4-5 minutes, or until most of the liquid has evaporated.
7.   Spoon cauliflower mixture onto plates, or in bowls, and top with mushrooms. Serve.

Prep
15 m

Portion
4

Cook
15 m

Per Serving
Calories: 178 fat: 11g Protein: 2g
Carbs: 18g

BRUSSELS SPROUT, AVOCADO, AND WILD RICE BOWL

. . . .

2 cups sliced Brussels sprouts
2 tsp extra-virgin olive oil, plus 2 tbsp
Juice of 1 lemon
1 tsp Dijon mustard
1 garlic clove, minced
½ tsp salt
¼ tsp freshly ground black pepper
1 cup cooked wild rice
1 cup sliced radishes
1 avocado, sliced

Directions:
1. Preheat the oven to 400°F. Line a baking sheet with parchment paper.
2. In a medium bowl, toss the Brussels sprouts with 2 tsp of olive oil and spread on the prepared baking sheet. Roast for 12 minutes, stirring once, until lightly browned. 3. In a small bowl, mix the remaining 2 tbsp of olive oil, lemon juice, mustard, garlic, salt, and pepper.
4. In a large bowl, toss the cooked wild rice, radishes, and roasted Brussels sprouts. Drizzle the dressing over the salad and toss.
5. Divide among 4 bowls and top with avocado slices.

Type 2 Diabetes Cookbook

Prep
15 m

Portion
2

Cook
20 m

Per Serving
Calories 441 Total Carbs 14g
Protein 24g Fat 35g

FIRENZE PIZZA

. . . .

1 3/4 cup grated mozzarella cheese
½ cup frozen spinach, thaw
1 egg
2 tbsp. reduced fat parmesan cheese, grated
2 tbsp. cream cheese, soft
What you'll need from the store cupboard
¾ cup almond flour
¼ cup light Alfredo sauce
½ tsp Italian seasoning
¼ tsp red pepper flakes
Pinch of salt

Directions:
1. Heat oven to 400 degrees.
2. Squeeze all the excess water out of the spinach.
3. In a glass bowl, combine mozzarella and almond flour. Stir in cream cheese. Microwave 1 minute on high, then stir. If the mixture is not melted, microwave another 30 seconds.
4. Stir in the egg, seasoning, and salt. Mix well. Place dough on a piece of parchment paper and press into a 10-inch circle.
5. Place directly on the oven rack and bake 8-10 minutes or until lightly browned.
6. Remove the crust and spread with the Alfredo sauce, then add spinach, parmesan and red pepper flakes evenly over top. Bake another 8-10 minutes. Slice and serve.

Prep
10 m

Portion
6

Cook
1 h

Per Serving
Calories 182 Carbs 5g Protein 10g
Fat

BROCCOLI QUICHE (NO-CRUST)

. . . .

3 large eggs
2 cups broccoli florets, chopped
1 small onion, diced
1 cup cheddar cheese, grated
2/3 cup unsweetened almond milk
½ cup feta cheese, crumbled
What you'll need from store cupboard:
1 tbsp. extra virgin olive oil
½ tsp sea salt
¼ tsp black pepper
Nonstick cooking spray

Directions:
1.　Heat oven to 350 degrees. Spray a 9-inch baking dish with cooking spray.
2.　Heat the oil in a large skillet over medium heat. Add onion and cook 4-5 minutes, until onions are translucent.
3.　Add broccoli and stir to combine. Cook until broccoli turns a bright green, about 2 minutes. Transfer to a bowl.
4.　In a small bowl, whisk together almond milk, egg, salt, and pepper. Pour over the broccoli. Add the cheddar cheese and stir the ingredients together. Pour into the prepared baking dish.
5.　Sprinkle the feta cheese over the top and bake 45 minutes to 1 hour, or until eggs are set in the middle and top is lightly browned. Serve.

Prep
2 m

Portion
4-6

Cook
5 m

Per Serving
Calories: 313; Fat: 14g; Carbs: 22g;
Protein: 13g

VEGAN THAI RED CURRY

. . . .

2 medium English cucumbers, spiralized
1 cup enoki mushroom
1 cup basil, roughly chopped
1 cup mint, roughly chopped
1 tbsp olive oil
1 medium red and green bell pepper, cut into bite-size pieces
1 scallion bunch, sliced, and discard the ends
2 medium eggplants, sliced
1 (4 oz) jar Thai red curry paste
½ cup peanuts, chopped
1 lime, quartered
Chili sauce or paste for serving

Directions:
1.   Place the spiraled cucumber noodles into a large deep bowl, and add the enoki, chopped basil, and chopped mint. Set aside.
2.   In a large wok, add the olive oil and place over high heat. Add the chopped red and green bell peppers, sliced scallions, and sliced eggplants and cook for 5 minutes, stirring often for the ingredients to color and not burn.
3.   Remove the wok from the heat and mix in the Thai red curry paste until all the vegetables are coated.
4.   Spoon the hot vegetables onto the cold cucumber noodles and garnish with peanuts, lime quarters and have the chili sauce or paste on the side.

Substitution tip: you can swap the cucumber noodles for zucchini noodles or use spaghetti squash.

Prep	**Portion**	**Cook**	**Per Serving**
10 m	4	45 m	142 fat: 4g Protein: 9g Carbs: 19g

MOZZARELLA AND ARTICHOKE STUFFED SPAGHETTI SQUASH

· ·

1 small spaghetti squash, halved and seeded
½ cup low-fat cottage cheese
¼ cup shredded mozzarella cheese, divided
2 garlic cloves, minced
1 cup artichoke hearts, chopped
1 cup thinly sliced kale
⅛ tsp salt
Pinch freshly ground black pepper

Directions

1. Preheat the oven to 400°F. Line a baking sheet with parchment paper.
2. Place the cut squash halves on the prepared baking sheet cut-side down, and roast for 30 to 40 minutes, depending on the size and thickness of the squash, until they are fork-tender. Set aside to cool slightly.
3. In a large bowl, mix the cottage cheese, 2 tbsp of mozzarella cheese, garlic, artichoke hearts, kale, salt, and pepper.
4. Preheat the broiler to high.
5. Using a fork, break apart the flesh of the spaghetti squash into strands, being careful to leave the skin intact. Add the strands to the cheese and vegetable mixture. Toss gently to combine.
6. Divide the mixture between the two hollowed-out squash halves and top with the remaining 2 tbsp of cheese.
7. Broil for 5 to 7 minutes until browned and heated through.
8. Cut each piece of stuffed squash in half to serve.

Prep	Portion	Cook	Per Serving
15 m	2	40 m	Calorie: 422 fat: 39g Protein: 8g Carbs: 17g

BEET, GOAT CHEESE, AND WALNUT PESTO WITH ZUCCHINI NOODLES

. . . .

1 medium red beet, peeled, chopped
½ cup walnut pieces
3 garlic cloves
½ cup crumbled goat cheese
2 tbsp extra-virgin olive oil, plus 2 tsp
2 tbsp freshly squeezed lemon juice
¼ tsp salt
4 small zucchini

Directions:
1.   Preheat the oven to 375°F.
2. Wrap the chopped beet in a piece of aluminum foil and seal well. Roast for 30 to 40 minutes until fork-tender.
3. Meanwhile, heat a dry skillet over medium-high heat. Toast the walnuts for 5 to 7 minutes until lightly browned and fragrant.
4. Transfer the cooked beets to the bowl of a food processor. Add the toasted walnuts, garlic, goat cheese, 2 tbsp of olive oil, lemon juice, and salt. Process until smooth. 5. Using a spiralizer or sharp knife, cut the zucchini into thin "noodles."
6. In a large skillet, heat the remaining 2 tsp of oil over medium heat. Add the zucchini and toss in the oil. Cook, stirring gently, for 2 to 3 minutes, until the zucchini softens. Toss with the beet pesto and serve warm.

Prep	Portion	Cook	Per Serving
5 m	4-6	15 m	Calories: 200; Fat: 13g; Carbs: 5g; Protein: 17g

SPINACH CASSEROLE

. . . .

1 lb. baby spinach
1 tbsp garlic, minced
Sea salt, fine
Black pepper, ground
4 large eggs
1 cup vegan parmesan, grated

Directions:

1. Heat the oven to 350°F gas mark 4.
2. Fill a medium cooking pot with water and bring to a boil. Add the baby spinach into the boiling water and let it cook for 30 seconds. Drain the spinach and place it in cold water immediately. Drain again and squeeze out any remaining water.
3. Place the spinach into a medium mixing bowl and mix in the minced garlic, fine sea salt, and ground black pepper to taste. Place the spinach into a deep casserole dish.
4. Flatten the top and then make 4 shallow dips in the spinach. Crack an egg into each dip. Sprinkle the eggs with vegan parmesan cheese.
5. Bake for 10 minutes, until the egg whites have set

Prep	Portion	Cook	Per Serving
5 m	4	10 m	Calories 113 Carbs 11g Protein 9g Fat 5g

PIZZA STUFFED WITH MUSHROOMS

. . . .

8 Portobello mushrooms, stems removed
1 cup mozzarella cheese, grated
1 cup cherry tomatoes, sliced
½ cup crushed tomatoes
½ cup fresh basil, chopped
What you'll need from store cupboard:
2 tbsp. balsamic vinegar
1 tbsp. olive oil
1 tbsp. oregano
1 tbsp. red pepper flakes
½ tbsp. garlic powder
¼ tsp pepper
Pinch salt

Directions:

1. Heat oven to broil. Line a baking sheet with foil.
2. Place mushrooms, stem side down, on foil and drizzle with oil. Sprinkle with garlic powder, salt and pepper. Broil for 5 minutes.
3. Flip mushrooms over and top with crushed tomatoes, oregano, parsley, pepper flakes, cheese and sliced tomatoes. Broil another 5 minutes.
4. Top with basil and drizzle with balsamic. Serve.

DESSERTS

SCAN ME! RECIPES' COLOR IMAGES

Prep
5 m

Portion
6

Cook
45 m

Per Serving
Calories: 184; Protein: 7g; Carbs:
9g; Fat: 16g

LOW-CARBS ALMOND CAKE

⅔ cup almond flour
⅓ cup applesauce, unsweetened
3 large eggs, separated
7 tbsp stevia sweetener, divided
3 tbsp organic butter, unsalted, melted, and divided
1 tsp vanilla extract or essence
¼ tsp almond extract
⅛ tsp sea salt, fine
½ cup almonds, sliced and toasted

Directions:

1. Preheat the oven to 350°F gas mark 4.
2. Brush a 7-inch cake pan with 1 tbsp of melted organic butter and sprinkle 1 tbsp of stevia sweetener to form a thin coating on the bottom. Set aside
3. In a stand mixer fitted with a paddle attachment, mix the almond flour, unsweetened applesauce, egg yolks, 3 tbsp of stevia sweetener, 2 tbsp of melted organic butter, vanilla extract or essence, almond extract, and fine sea salt, until well combined.
4. In a medium bowl, using a hand mixer, beat the egg whites for 3 to 5 minutes, until soft peaks have formed, add and whisk in 3 tbsp of stevia sweetener.
5. Using a silicone spatula, gently fold the egg whites into the yolk mixture until well combined. Pour the batter into the prepared cake pan.
6. Bake for 45 minutes, or until the top is lightly browned and a toothpick inserted into the middle comes out clean.
7. Let the cake cool on a cooling rack.
8. In the meantime, scatter the sliced almonds onto a microwave-safe plate and microwave for 1½ minutes to toast. Sprinkle the toasted almonds on the cooled cake.

Tip: You can dust the cake with powdered sugar and add some fresh berries or make a berry compote.

Prep
15 m

Portion
4-6

Cook
3 m

Per Serving
Calories: 254; Fat: 22g; Carbs: 13g;
Protein: 7g

VEGAN CHEESECAKE BITES (NO-BAKED)

. . . .

½ cup almond flour
¼ cup almonds, sliced
¼ tsp kosher salt, fine
1 (8-oz) package cream cheese, vegan
3 tbsp sweetener, any of your choice
2 lemons, zested
⅛ tsp vanilla extract

Directions:
1. Place the almond flour into a microwave-safe container and microwave for 1½ min to lightly toast it, set aside to cool. Repeat the same method with the sliced almonds.
2. Add the fine kosher salt into the cooled, toasted almond flour.
3. In a medium mixing bowl, add the vegan cream cheese, sweetener, lemon zest, and vanilla extract and mix until combined.
4. Spoon 1 tbsp of the cream cheese mixture and roll it in the almond flour to coat and set it on a plate.

Repeat the same method with the remaining cream cheese mixture.
5. Place 3 or 4 toasted almond slices on top of each bite. Serve right away or place in the fridge for 1 hour and serve chilled.

Prep
5 m

Portion
16 Makes

Cook
15m

Per Serving
76 fat: 6g Protein: 2g Carbs: 5g

OATMEAL COOKIES

minutes. 5. Using a spatula, remove the cookies and cool on a rack.

¾ cup almond flour
¾ cup old-fashioned oats
¼ cup shredded unsweetened coconut
1 tsp baking powder
1 tsp ground cinnamon
¼ tsp salt
¼ cup unsweetened applesauce
1 large egg
1 tbsp pure maple syrup
2 tbsp coconut oil, melted

Directions

1. Preheat the oven to 350°F. 2. In a medium mixing bowl, combine the almond flour, oats, coconut, baking powder, cinnamon, and salt, and mix well. 3. In another medium bowl, combine the applesauce, egg, maple syrup, and coconut oil, and mix. Stir the wet mixture into the dry mixture. 4. Form the dough into balls a little bigger than a tbsp and place on a baking sheet, leaving at least 1 inch between them. Bake for 12 minutes until the cookies are just browned. Remove from the oven and let cool for 5

Type 2 Diabetes Cookbook

Prep
5 m

Portion
8

Cook
35 m

Per Serving
Calories 375 Carbs 20g Protein 7g
Fat 30g

CARAMEL PECAN PIE

1 cup pecans, chopped
¾ cup almond milk, unsweetened
1/3 cup margarine, melted
1 tbsp. margarine, cold
What you'll need from the store cupboard
2 cup almond flour
½ cup + 2 tbsp Splenda for baking
1 tsp vanilla
1 tsp Arrowroot powder
¾ tsp sea salt
½ tsp vanilla
½ tsp maple syrup, sugar free
Non-stick cooking spray

Directions:
1.   Heat oven to 350 degrees. Spray a 9-inch pie pan with cooking spray.
2.   In a medium bowl, combine flour, melted margarine, 2 tbsp Splenda, and vanilla. Mix to thoroughly combine Ingredients. Press on bottom and sides of prepared pie pan. Bake 12 -15 minutes, or until edges start to brown. Set aside.

3.   In a small sauce pan, combine milk, remaining Splenda, arrowroot, salt, ½ tsp vanilla, and syrup. Cook over medium heat until it starts to boil, stirring constantly. Keep cooking until it turns a gold color and starts to thicken, about 2-3 minutes. Remove from heat and let cool. Stir in ½ the pecans.
4.   Pour the filling in the crust and top with remaining pecans. Bake about 15 minutes, or until filling starts to bubble. Cool completely before serving.

Prep
10 m

Portion
12 Makes

Cook
35 m

Per Serving
Calories 160 Carbs 13g Protein 4g
Fat 10g

CARROT CUPCAKES

2 cup carrots, grated
1 cup low fat cream cheese, soft
2 eggs
1-2 tsp skim milk
What you'll need from store cupboard:
½ cup coconut oil, melted
¼ cup coconut flour
¼ cup Splenda (sweetener)
¼ cup honey
2 tsp vanilla, divided
1 tsp baking powder
1 tsp cinnamon
Non-stick cooking spray

Directions:
1.   Heat oven to 350 degrees. Lightly spray a muffin pan with cooking spray, or use paper liners.
2.   In a large bowl, stir together the flour, baking powder, and cinnamon.
3.   Add the carrots, eggs, oil, Splenda, and vanilla to a food processor. Process until Ingredients are combined but carrots still have some large chunks remaining. Add to dry Ingredients and stir to combine.
4.   Pour evenly into prepared pan, filling cups 2/3 full. Bake 30-35 minutes, or until cupcakes pass the toothpick test. Remove from oven and let cool.
5.   In a medium bowl, beat cream cheese, honey, and vanilla on high speed until smooth. Add milk, one tsp at a time, beating after each addition, until frosting is creamy enough to spread easily.
6.   Once cupcakes have cooled, spread each one with about 2 tbsp of frosting. Chill until ready to serve.

Prep	**Portion**	**Cook**	**Per Serving**
5 m	12 Makes	30 m	80 Calories, 6g fat, 6g Carbs, 1g Protein

POMEGRANATE AND NUT CHOCOLATE CLUSTERS

⅓ cup pecans, toasted and chopped
¼ cup shelled pistachios, toasted and chopped
2 tbsp unsweetened flaked coconut, toasted
2 tbsp pomegranate seeds
3 ounces semisweet chocolate, chopped fine

Directions:
1.   Line rimmed baking sheet with parchment paper. Combine pecans, pistachios, coconut, and pomegranate seeds in bowl.
2.   Microwave 2 ounces chocolate in bowl at 50 percent power, stirring often, until about two-thirds melted, 45 to 60 seconds. Remove bowl from microwave; stir in remaining 1 ounce chocolate until melted. If necessary, microwave chocolate at 50 percent power for 5 seconds at a time until melted.
3.   Working quickly, measure 1 tsp melted chocolate onto prepared sheet and spread into 2½-inch wide circle using back of spoon. Repeat with remaining chocolate, spacing circles 1½ inches apart.
4.   Sprinkle pecan mixture evenly over chocolate and press gently to adhere. Refrigerate until chocolate is firm, about 30 minutes. Serve.

Tip: If you don't have a microwave, you can melt chocolate on a plate by putting a pot with boiling water under it.

Prep
15 m

Portion
14 Makes

Cook
25 m

Per Serving
Calories 260 Carbs 12g Protein 5g Fat 21g

COFFEE BAKE

. . . .

8 eggs
1 cup margarine, cut into cubes
What you'll need from store cupboard:
1 lb. bittersweet chocolate, chopped
¼ cup brewed coffee, room temperature
Non-stick cooking spray

Directions:

1.   Heat oven to 325 degrees. Spray an 8-inch springform pan with cooking spray. Line bottom of sides with parchment paper and spray again. Wrap the outside with a double layer of foil and place in 9x13-inch baking dish. Put a small saucepan of water on to boil.

2.   In a large bowl, beat the eggs on med speed until doubled in volume, about 5 minutes.

3.   Place the chocolate, margarine and coffee into microwave safe bowl and microwave on high, until chocolate is melted and mixture is smooth, stir every 30 seconds.

4.   Fold 1/3 of the eggs into chocolate mixture until almost combined. Add the remaining eggs, 1/3 at a time and fold until combined.

5.   Pour into prepared pan. Pour boiling water around the springform pan until it reaches halfway up the sides. Bake 22-25 minutes, or until cake has risen slightly and edges are just beginning to set.

6.   Remove from water bath and let cool completely. Cover with plastic wrap and chill 6 hours or overnight. About 30 minutes before serving, run a knife around the edges and remove the side of the pan. Slice and serve.

Prep
5 m

Portion
12 Makes

Cook
15 m

Per Serving
(1 brownie): calorie: 170 fat: 10gProtein: 3g Carbs: 19g

PEANUT BUTTER FUDGE BROWNIES

. . . .

Cooking oil spray, as needed
1 cup (80 g) gluten-free rolled oats
½ cup (48 g) almond flour
1 cup (194 g) canned low-sodium black beans, drained and rinsed
¼ cup (60 ml) cooking oil of choice
1½ tsp (8 ml) pure vanilla extract
¼ tsp baking soda
1 tsp baking powder
¼ tsp sea salt
1 tsp ground cinnamon
⅓ cup (32 g) unsweetened cocoa powder
½ cup (120 ml) pure maple syrup
¼ cup (45 g) dairy-free dark chocolate chips
2 tbsp (30 g) all-natural peanut butter (see Tip)

Directions:

1. Preheat the oven to 350°F (177°C). Spray an 8 x 8–inch (20 x 20–cm) baking pan with the cooking oil spray.
2. In a food processor, combine the oats, almond flour, beans, oil, vanilla, baking soda, baking powder, sea salt, cinnamon, cocoa powder, and maple syrup. Process the ingredients for about 1 minute, until the batter is smooth. You may need to stop the food processor once and scrape down the sides.
3. Carefully remove the food processor's blade and stir in the chocolate chips by hand.
4. Spread the batter into the prepared baking pan. Drizzle the peanut butter over the top of the batter.
5. Bake the brownies for 15 minutes, until a toothpick inserted into the center comes out clean. Let the brownies cool completely in the pan on a wire rack.

Prep	**Portion**	**Cook**	**Per Serving**
5 m	1	20 m	72 Calories, 4g fat, 10g Carbs., 1g Protein

FROZEN CHOCOLATE MONKEY TREATS

. . . .

3 medium bananas
1 cup (6 ounces) dark chocolate chips
2 tsp shortening
Toppings: chopped peanuts, toasted flaked coconut and/or colored jimmies

Directions:

1.　Cut each banana into six pieces (about 1 in.). Insert a toothpick into each piece; transfer to a waxed paper-lined baking sheet. Freeze until completely firm, about 1 hour.

2.　In a microwave, melt chocolate and shortening; stir until smooth. Dip banana pieces in chocolate mixture; allow excess to drip off. Dip in toppings as desired; return to baking sheet. Freeze 30 minutes before serving.
 set

Prep	**Portion**	**Cook**	**Per Serving**
5 m	8	1h 30 m	Calories: 347; Fat: 28g; Carbs: 14g; Protein: 12g

PISTACHIO AND RICOTTA CHEESECAKE

. . . .

Non-stick cooking spray
1½ cups pistachio nuts, roasted
4 tbsp butter, unsalted
1 cup fat-free ricotta cheese
8 oz fat-free cream cheese
¾ cup sweetener, any of your choice
2 eggs, beaten
2 tsp vanilla extract
2 tbsp coconut flour
1 tsp sea salt, fine
1 medium lemon, juiced
½ cup cherries, pitted

Directions:

1.　Preheat the oven to 350°F gas mark 4. Coat a 9-inch springform pan with non-stick cooking spray.

2.　Pulse the pistachios and butter in a food processor, until fine crumbs form.

3.　Press the pistachio mixture into the bottom of the prepared pan and set it aside.

4.　In a stand mixer, combine the fat-free ricotta, fat-free cream cheese, sweetener, beaten eggs, vanilla extract, coconut flour, and fine sea salt and mix well for 3 minutes, add the lemon juice.

5.　Pour half of the filling on top of the crust in the springform pan, layer with pitted cherries and pour the remainder of the filling on top.

6.　Bake for 1 hour.

7.　Remove from the oven, set it on a cooling rack to cool to room temperature, and then refrigerate for a few hours or overnight before removing the cheesecake out of the springform pan and serving.

Tip: place a deep dish smaller than the inside of your oven, filled halfway with hot water. This will prevent your cheesecake from cracking in the center.

Prep	**Portion**	**Cook**	**Per Serving**
15 m	12 MAKES	0 m	Calories: 101 fat: 8g Protein: 3g Carbs: 6g

DARK CHOCOLATE ALMOND BUTTER CUPS

. . . .

½ cup natural almond butter
1 tbsp pure maple syrup
1 cup dark chocolate chips
1 tbsp coconut oil

Directions

1.   Line a 12-cup muffin tin with cupcake liners.
2. In a medium bowl, mix the almond butter and maple syrup. If necessary, heat in the microwave to soften slightly.
3. Spoon about 2 tsp of the almond butter mixture into each muffin cup and press down to fill.
4. In a double boiler or the microwave, melt the chocolate chips. Stir in the coconut oil, and mix well to incorporate.
5. Drop 1 tbsp of chocolate on top of each almond butter cup.
6. Freeze for at least 30 minutes to set. Thaw for 10 minutes before serving.

Prep	**Portion**	**Cook**	**Per Serving**
10 m	12 Makes	20 m	Calories: 84 fat: 6g Protein: 2g Carbs: 6g

SWIRLED CREAM CHEESE BROWNIES

. . . .

2 eggs
¼ cup unsweetened applesauce
¼ cup coconut oil, melted
3 tbsp pure maple syrup, divided
¼ cup unsweetened cocoa powder
¼ cup coconut flour
¼ tsp salt
1 tsp baking powder
2 tbsp low-fat cream cheese

Directions:

1.   Preheat the oven to 350°F (180°C). Grease an 8-by-8-inch baking dish.
2. In a large mixing bowl, beat the eggs with the applesauce, coconut oil, and 2 tbsp of maple syrup.
3. Stir in the cocoa powder and coconut flour, and mix well. Sprinkle the salt and baking powder evenly over the surface and mix well to incorporate. Transfer the mixture to the prepared baking dish.
4. In a small, microwave-safe bowl, microwave the cream cheese for 10 to 20 seconds until softened. Add the remaining 1 tbsp of maple syrup and mix to combine.
5. Drop the cream cheese onto the batter, and use a toothpick or chopstick to swirl it on the surface. Bake for 20 minutes, until a toothpick inserted in the center comes out clean. Cool and cut into 12 squares.
6. Store refrigerated in a covered container for up to 5 days.

Prep	Portion	Cook	Per Serving
45 m	MAKES 5 DOZEN COOKIES	8-10 m	(1 Cookie): calorie: 45 fat: 1g Protein: 0g Carbs: 9g

DOUBLE-GINGER COOKIES

. . . .

¾ cup sugar
¼ cup butter or margarine, softened
1 egg or ¼ cup fat-free egg product
¼ cup molasses
1¾ cups all-purpose flour
1 tsp baking soda
½ tsp ground cinnamon
½ tsp ground ginger
¼ tsp ground cloves
¼ tsp salt
¼ cup sugar
¼ cup orange marmalade
2 tbsp finely chopped crystallized ginger

Directions

1. In medium bowl, beat ¾ cup sugar, the butter, egg and molasses with electric mixer on medium speed, or mix with spoon. Stir in flour, baking soda, cinnamon, ground ginger, cloves and salt. Cover and refrigerate at least 2 hours, until firm.
2. Heat oven to 350°F. Lightly spray cookie sheets with cooking spray. Place ¼ cup sugar in small bowl. Shape dough into ¾-inch balls; roll in sugar. Place balls about 2 inches apart on cookie sheet. Make indentation in center of each ball, using finger. Fill each indentation with slightly less than ¼ tsp of the marmalade. Sprinkle with crystallized ginger.
3. Bake 8 to 10 minutes or until set. Immediately transfer from cookie sheets to cooling racks. Cool completely, about 30 minutes.

Prep	Portion	Cook	Per Serving
5 m	4	20 m	(1 pear half): Calories: 91; Fat: 3g; Protein: 2g; Carbs: 15g

PEAR AND CINNAMON BAKE

. . . .

2 pears, halved lengthwise and cored
¼ cup almond flour
2 tbsp rolled oats
1 tsp maple syrup
½ tsp cinnamon, ground
Pinch sea salt, fine

Directions:

1. Preheat the oven to 350°F gas mark 4.
2. Place the pear halves, cut side up, in a square baking dish.
3. In a small mixing bowl, combine the almond flour, rolled oats, maple syrup, ground cinnamon, and fine sea salt and mix well. Add the filling into the pear halves.
4. Bake the pears for 20 minutes until tender and the filling is golden, serve warm.

CONCLUSIONS

Congratulations on making the healthy choice to change your diet. Combining dietary changes with medication prescribed by your doctor is a recipe for success. Being diagnosed with type 2 diabetes can bring down the wind from your sails. You've lost something important to you: your health.

At first, you may deny it, looking for a second opinion or something else that may have caused your high blood sugar. And then you may have felt angry at yourself or your parents for giving you the genes that predispose you to the condition. Bargaining comes later. If you quit sugar for good, maybe diabetes will go away. When you realize it's here to stay, depression may creep in. But in the end, you find yourself where you are today - accepting your diagnosis and planning the rest of your life.

That's the advantage this beginner's cookbook has over every other diabetes cookbook—the freedom to eat healthy foods and eat the best at the same time. Coming up with a healthy diabetic diet doesn't have to be mind-boggling, and You don't get to give up all your favorite foods because you have diabetes. The first step to making healthier and smarter choices is to make lifestyle changes through a healthy diet, healthy living, and exercise. Follow the 28-day eating plan in this book and eat more natural, unprocessed foods and less packaged, convenient foods to enjoy good health.

APPEAL FROM THE PUBLISHER

Hello, fantastic reader!
I hope you are enjoying this book.

I just thought you should know you have improved not only your life but some other lives by reading this book.

I introduce myself and my team: We are a small publishing company with a team of six members (2 writers (me and my husband), 2 editors, and 2 designers).
Most of our employees come from lower-income sectors, and our business is the only way to provide for their families. It is a way for us to give back to society.

We don't have the enormous advertising budgets that many other publishers and businesses do Online.
So, you can really support our mission and our business by leaving us a review in this book.
Review now on:
http://www.amazon.com/review/create-review?&asin=

For a small company like us, getting reviews (especially on Amazon) means the possibility to submit our books for advertising. It also means we can just sell a few copies once in a while and have a more meaningful effect on society as a whole. So, every review means a lot to us.

We can't THANK YOU enough for this!

Important Notice: <u>We take seriously customer suggestion</u>. If you have any, please write to:
et.publishing.us@gmail.com writing in the email object the book's title, or
USE THE QR CODE BELOW TO TAKE A SHORT SURVEY AND HELP US IMPROVE THE BOOK QUALITY.

Thank You for Reading This Book.
If You Enjoyed It, Please Visit the Site Where You
Purchased It and Write A Brief Review. Your Feedback Is
Important to Me and Will Help Other Readers Decide
Whether to Read the Book Too.
Thank You
Julia Martin

conversion chart
FOR THE KITCHEN

Cups	Tablespoons	Teaspoons	Milliliters
		1 tsp	5 ml
1/16 cup	1 tbsp	3 tsp	15 ml
1/8 cup	2 tbsp	6 tsp	30 ml
1/4 cup	4 tbsp	12 tsp	60 ml
1/3 cup	5 1/3 tbsp	16 tsp	80 ml
1/2 cup	8 tbsp	24 tsp	120 ml
2/3 cup	10 2/3 tbsp	32 tsp	160 ml
3/4 cup	12 tbsp	36 tsp	180 ml
1 cup	16 tbsp	48 tsp	240 ml

1 QUART =
2 pints
4 cups
32 ounces
950 ml

1 PINT =
2 cups
16 ounces
480 ml

1 CUP =
16 tbsp
8 ounces
240 ml

1/4 CUP =
4 tbsp
12 tsp
2 ounces
60 ml

1 TBSP =
3 tsp
1/2 ounce
15 ml

COOKING TEMPERATURE CONVERSIONS

Celcius/Centigrade	F= (C x 1.8) + 32
Fahrenheit	C= (F-32) x 0.5556

Type 2 Diabetes Cookbook

BAKING INGREDIENT CONVERSIONS

BUTTER

Cups	Grams
1/4 cup	57 grams
1/3 cup	76 grams
1/2 cup	113 grams
1 cup	227 grams

PACKED BROWN SUGAR

Cups	Grams	Ounces
1/4 cup	55 grams	1.9 oz
1/3 cup	73 grams	2.58 oz
1/2 cup	110 grams	3.88 oz
1 cup	220 grams	7.75 oz

ALL-PURPOSE FLOUR \ CONFECTIONER'S SUGAR

Cups	Grams	Ounces
1/8 cup	16 grams	.563 oz
1/4 cup	32 grams	1.13 oz
1/3 cup	43 grams	1.5 oz
1/2 cup	64 grams	2.25 oz
2/3 cup	85 grams	3 oz
3/4 cup	96 grams	3.38 oz
1 cup	128 grams	4.5 oz

GRANULATED SUGAR

Cups	Grams	Ounces
2 tbsp	25 grams	.89 oz
1/4 cup	50 grams	1.78 oz
1/3 cup	67 grams	2.37 oz
1/2 cup	100 grams	3.55 oz
2/3 cup	134 grams	4.73 oz
3/4 cup	150 grams	5.3 oz
1 cup	201 grams	7.1 oz

1350214b-b7c2-4b1a-b324-fe03bc370336R01